W9-AZK-095

Fix It Fast

DINNER READY
IN 25 MINUTES OR LESS

WILEY

WILEY PUBLISHING, INC.

Copyright © 2005 by General Mills, Inc., Minneapolis, MN. All rights reserved.

Published by Wiley Publishing, Inc., Hoboken, NJ

No part of this publication may be reproduced, stored in a retrieval system or transmitted in any form or by any means, electronic, mechanical, photocopying, recording, scanning or otherwise, except as permitted under Sections 107 or 108 of the 1976 United States Copyright Act, without either the prior written permission of the Publisher, or authorization through payment of the appropriate per-copy fee to the Copyright Clearance Center, 222 Rosewood Drive, Danvers, MA 01923, (978) 750-8400, fax (978) 646-8600. Requests to the Publisher for permission should be addressed to the Legal Department, Wiley Publishing, Inc., 10475 Crosspoint Blvd., Indianapolis, IN 46256, (317) 572-3447, fax (317) 572-4447, E-Mail: permcoordinator@wiley.com.

Trademarks: Wiley and the Wiley Publishing logo are trademarks or registered trademarks of John Wiley & Sons and/or its affiliates. All other trademarks referred to herein are trademarks of General Mills. Wiley Publishing, Inc., is not associated with any product or vendor mentioned in this book.

Limit of Liability/Disclaimer of Warranty: While the publisher and author have used their best efforts in preparing this book, they make no representations or warranties with respect to the accuracy or completeness of the contents of this book and specifically disclaim any implied warranties of merchantability or fitness for a particular purpose. No warranty may be created or extended by sales representatives or written sales materials. The advice and strategies contained herein may not be suitable for your situation. You should consult with a professional where appropriate. Neither the publisher nor author shall be liable for any loss of profit or any other commercial damages, including but not limited to special, incidental, consequential, or other damages.

For general information on our other products and services or to obtain technical support please contact our Customer Care Department within the U.S. at 800-762-2974, outside the U.S. at 317-572-3993 or fax 317-572-4002.

Wiley also publishes its books in a variety of electronic formats. Some content that appears in print may not be available in electronic books.

Library of Congress Cataloging-in-Publication Data:

Pillsbury fix it fast / [editor, Lois L. Tlusty].
   p. cm.
  Includes index.

     ISBN-13 978-0-7645-8814-3
     ISBN-10- 0-7645-8814-1(hc. : alk. paper)
1. Quick and easy cookery. I. Tlusty, Lois L. II. Pillsbury Company.
  TX833.5.P553 2005
  641.5'55--dc22

                     2005012584

Manufactured in China

10 9 8 7 6 5 4 3 2 1

Cover photo: Stand-Up Chicken Tacos (page 23)

General Mills

DIRECTOR, BOOK AND ONLINE PUBLISHING:
Kim Walter

MANAGER, COOKBOOK PUBLISHING:
Lois Tlusty

EDITOR:
Lois Tlusty

RECIPE DEVELOPMENT AND TESTING:
Pillsbury Kitchens

PHOTOGRAPHY AND FOOD STYLING:
General Mills Photography Studios and Image Library

Wiley Publishing, Inc.

PUBLISHER:
Natalie Chapman

EXECUTIVE EDITOR:
Anne Ficklen

EDITOR:
Kristi Hart

PRODUCTION DIRECTOR:
Diana Cisek

COVER DESIGN:
Paul DiNovo

INTERIOR DESIGN AND LAYOUT:
Lee Goldstein

MANUFACTURING MANAGER:
Kevin Watt

Home of the Pillsbury Bake-Off® Contest

Our recipes have been tested in the Pillsbury Kitchens and meet our standards of easy preparation, reliability and great taste.

For more great recipes, visit pillsbury.com

Welcome...

From the Pillsbury Kitchens
Home of the Pillsbury Bake-Off® Contest

If you'd like your family's mealtime focus to be on the family instead of the time it takes to pull a meal together, you've come to the right place.

Feeding your family day in and day out is not an easy job. When you've got busy schedules to juggle and finicky palates to please and you don't want to serve the same old foods week after week, the task can seem daunting.

We can help. Pillsbury Fix It Fast is chock full of family-pleasing recipes, each of which can be made in 25 minutes—some even less! From fresh and filling sandwiches and main-dish salads, to hot and hearty pastas, skillet dishes and soups, this cookbook is an indispensable resource for busy families.

In addition to super-fast family friendly recipes, we've also included 20 delicious menu ideas to help you plan meals. Look for color-packed pages throughout that offer clever ways to use things you already have in your kitchen. Who knew a wire cooling rack, ice cube trays and plastic food-storage bags could be so versatile?

Life is complicated. Getting a great-tasting meal on the table your family will love shouldn't be.

The Pillsbury Editors

Contents

Easy Family Sandwiches

Superfast Ready in 15 minutes or less

Sloppy Joe Confetti Tacos

■ ■ ■ ■ **Ready in 20 minutes**

6 servings (2 tacos each)

1 lb. lean (at least 80%) ground beef
1 package (4.6 oz.) taco shells (12 shells)
1 can (15.5 oz.) sloppy joe sauce
1 small red bell pepper, chopped
1 can (11 oz.) vacuum-packed whole kernel corn, drained
1 can (2 1/4 oz.) sliced ripe olives, drained
1 cup thinly sliced romaine lettuce
1/2 cup shredded Colby-Monterey Jack cheese (2 oz.)

1. Heat oven to 350°F. In 10-inch skillet, cook ground beef over medium-high heat for 5 to 7 minutes or until thoroughly cooked, stirring frequently. Drain.

2. Meanwhile, heat taco shells as directed on package.

3. Stir sloppy joe sauce, bell pepper and corn into ground beef. Cook an additional 2 to 3 minutes or until mixture is hot and bubbly.

4. Spoon about 1/4 cup beef mixture into each warm taco shell. Top each with olives, lettuce and cheese.

1 SERVING
Calories 495 (Calories from Fat 260); Total Fat 29g (Saturated Fat 11g); Cholesterol 90mg; Sodium 860mg; Total Carbohydrates 30g (Dietary Fiber 3g); Sugars 6g; Protein 29g

% Daily Value: Vitamin A 28%; Vitamin C 30%; Calcium 12%; Iron 22%

Exchanges: 2 Starch, 3 1/2 Medium–Fat Meat, 2 Fat

Carbohydrate Choices: 2

QUICK FIX
Make ths a "no-chop" recipe. Look for packages of frozen chopped bell pepper near the frozen vegetables, and purchase a bag of torn or shredded romaine lettuce in the produce department.

Open-Faced Hamburger Philly's
Tomato Dill Soup
Potato Chips
Green Grapes

4 servings

1 Cook ground beef mixture for sandwiches. Heat the broiler.

2 While the ground beef mixture cooks, make the soup.

3 Toast bread and make sandwiches.

4 Serve with potato chips and grapes.

Tomato Dill Soup

2 cans (10.75 oz.) condensed tomato soup
1/2 to 1 cup nonfat plain yogurt
3/4 cup water
1/2 cup half-and-half
1 teaspoon dried dill

1 In medium saucepan, combine all ingredients.

2 Cook over medium heat, stirring occasionally, until thoroughly heated. (Do not boil because it may curdle.)

1 SERVING

Calories 170 (Calories from Fat 50);
Total Fat 6g (Saturated Fat 3g);
Cholesterol 10mg; Sodium 940mg;
Total Carbohydrates 26g (Dietary Fiber 1g); Sugars 12g; Protein 5g
% Daily Value: Vitamin A 15%;
Vitamin C 20%; Calcium 10%; Iron 6%
Exchanges: 1 1/2 Starch, 1 Fat
Carbohydrate Choices: 2

QUICK FIX

There is a range for the amount of yogurt so you can use the amount that suits your taste. The more yogurt you use, the tangier the soup.

Open-Faced Hamburger Philly's

1 lb. lean (at least 80%) ground beef
1 medium green bell pepper, cut into 1/2-inch strips
1 medium red bell pepper, cut into 1/2-inch strips
1 small onion, cut into thin wedges
1/2 cup creamy Italian salad dressing
1 loaf (1 lb.) Italian bread (12 inches long)
1 package (8 oz.) thinly sliced provolone cheese

1. In 10-inch skillet, cook ground beef, bell peppers and onion over medium-high heat for 5 to 7 minutes or until beef is thoroughly cooked, stirring frequently. Drain. Stir in 1/4 cup of the salad dressing. Remove skillet from heat.

2. Cut Italian bread in half horizontally. Spread remaining 1/4 cup salad dressing on cut sides of bread. Place both halves, cut sides up, on ungreased large cookie sheet. Broil 4 to 6 inches from heat for 1 to 2 minutes or until lightly toasted.

3. Remove bread from broiler. Spread beef mixture on cut halves of bread. Top with cheese.

4. Return to broiler; broil 4 to 6 inches from heat for 2 to 3 minutes or until cheese is melted. Cut each half into 2 pieces.

1 SANDWICH

Calories 880 (Calories from Fat 432);
Total Fat 48g (Saturated Fat 18g);
Cholesterol 120mg; Sodium 1,530mg;
Total Carbohydrates 66g (Dietary
Fiber 4g); Sugars 8g; Protein 46g
% Daily Value: Vitamin A 49%;
Vitamin C 70%; Calcium 54%; Iron 32%
Exchanges: 4 1/2 Starch, 4 1/2 Medium-
Fat Meat, 5 Fat
Carbohydrate Choices: 4 1/2

QUICK FIX

Fast is the name of the game when you substitute about 2 1/2 cups frozen bell pepper and onion stir-fry mixture for the bell peppers and onion. Look for this time-saving product near the other frozen vegetables.

Chicken, Vegetable and Cream Cheese Sandwiches *Superfast*

Ready in 10 minutes

4 sandwiches

8 slices pumpernickel rye bread
1 container (6.5 oz.) gourmet spreadable cheese with garlic and
 herbs (1 cup)
16 thin slices cucumber
1 lb. sliced cooked chicken (from deli)
1 medium tomato, sliced
1 slice (1/4 inch thick) sweet onion (Walla Walla, Maui or Texas
 Sweet), separated into rings
1 cup coleslaw mix (from 16-oz. bag)

1. Spread one side of all slices of bread with gourmet spreadable cheese.
2. Top 4 bread slices, cheese side up, evenly with cucumber, chicken, tomato, onion and coleslaw mix. Cover with remaining bread slices, cheese side down.

1 SANDWICH

Calories 480 (Calories from Fat 250);
Total Fat 28g (Saturated Fat 13g);
Cholesterol 95mg; Sodium 2,040mg;
Total Carbohydrates 34g (Dietary
Fiber 4g); Sugars 7g; Protein 23g

% Daily Value: Vitamin A 20%;
Vitamin C 22%; Calcium 10%; Iron 16%

Exchanges: 2 Starch, 2 1/2 Lean Meat, 4 Fat

Carbohydrate Choices: 2

QUICK FIX

Everyone on a different schedule? You'll feel good when you have these tasty sandwiches in the refrigerator, wrapped and ready to eat for family members who are on the go!

Chicken, Vegetable and
Cream Cheese Sandwiches

Barbecue Chicken Wraps

■ ■ ■ ■ **Ready in 20 minutes**   *4 wraps*

2 cups refrigerated original barbecue sauce with shredded
    chicken (from 18-oz. container)
4 slices precooked bacon (from 2.1- or 2.8-oz. package), cut into
    pieces, if desired
4 flour tortillas (10 to 12 inch), heated
1 cup shredded Cheddar cheese (4 oz.)
1 cup creamy coleslaw

1 In 1-quart saucepan, cook barbecue sauce with shredded
   chicken and bacon over medium heat for 5 to 10 minutes or
   until thoroughly heated, stirring occasionally.

2 Spoon 1/2 cup chicken mixture down center of each warm
   tortilla. Top each with cheese. Spoon coleslaw down sides of
   each. Fold up bottom of each tortilla; fold in sides. If desired,
   enclose bottom of wraps in foil or waxed paper.

1 WRAP

Calories 620 (Calories from Fat 240);
Total Fat 27g (Saturated Fat 9g);
Cholesterol 75mg; Sodium 1,540mg;
Total Carbohydrates 65g
(Dietary Fiber 3g); Sugars 15g; Protein 29g

% Daily Value: Vitamin A 15%;
Vitamin C 8%; Calcium 35%; Iron 30%

Exchanges: 3 1/2 Starch, 2 1/2 Lean Meat,
3 1/2 Fat, 1 Other Carbohydrate

Carbohydrate Choices: 4

QUICK FIX

Want to make just one wrap at a time? Sprinkle the bacon over the chicken in sauce, and
store in the refrigerator with the other ingredients. Scoop about 1/2 cup mixture into a
microwavable container, then microwave on High for 1 to 1 1/2 minutes or until hot. Make
individual wraps as directed in the recipe.

California Club Biscuit Sandwiches

■ ■ ■ ■ **Ready in 20 minutes**

5 sandwiches

1 can (10.2 oz.) large refrigerated buttermilk homestyle
    biscuits (5 biscuits)
1 package (9 oz.) frozen cooked chicken breast strips
5 tablespoons ranch salad dressing
5 slices precooked bacon (from 2.1- or 2.8-oz. package)
5 tomato slices
5 slices cooked ham (.75 oz.)
5 lettuce leaves

1 Heat oven to 375°F. Separate dough into 5 biscuits; split each
into 2 rounds. Press or roll each round into 4-inch round;
place on ungreased cookie sheets. Bake for 7 to 9 minutes or
until golden brown.

2 Meanwhile, heat chicken strips in microwave as directed on
package.

3 Spread about 1 1/2 teaspoons salad dressing on each warm
biscuit half. Top 5 biscuit halves with chicken strips, bacon,
tomato, ham and lettuce. Cover with remaining biscuit halves.

1 SANDWICH

Calories 380 (Calories from Fat 190);
Total Fat 21g (Saturated Fat 5g);
Cholesterol 50mg; Sodium 1,290mg; Total
Carbohydrates 26g (Dietary Fiber 1g);
Sugars 5g; Protein 22g

% Daily Value: Vitamin A 6%;
Vitamin C 4%; Calcium 4%; Iron 10%

Exchanges: 1 1/2 Starch, 2 1/2 Lean Meat,
2 1/2 Fat

Carbohydrate Choices: 2

QUICK FIX

Keep refrigerated biscuits on hand for great hearty sandwiches like these. For the best
results, store the can of dough in the coldest part of the refrigerator until just before
baking.

Mediterranean Chicken Focaccia

6 servings

1 round loaf (1 lb.) focaccia bread
1/4 cup mayonnaise
1/4 cup basil pesto
2 medium tomatoes, sliced
4 slices mozzarella or provolone cheese
1 medium green bell pepper, sliced
1 thin slice red onion, separated into rings
2 cups shredded cooked chicken (from deli rotisserie chicken)

1. Cut focaccia bread in half horizontally. In small bowl, blend mayonnaise and pesto. Spread on cut surfaces of focaccia bread.
2. Layer bottom half of focaccia bread with tomatoes, cheese, bell pepper and onion. Place chicken on top of vegetables. Cover with top half of focaccia bread; press down lightly. Cut into wedges.

1 SERVING
Calories 505 (Calories from Fat 245);
Total Fat 27g (Saturated Fat 6g);
Cholesterol 55mg; Sodium 990mg;
Total Carbohydrates 40g
(Dietary Fiber 2g); Sugars 3g;
Protein 25g

% Daily Value: Vitamin A 12%;
Vitamin C 20%; Calcium 20%; Iron 18%

Exchanges: 2 1/2 Starch, 2 1/2 Lean Meat, 4 Fat

Carbohydrate Choices: 2 1/2

QUICK FIX

Pick up potato salad at the deli to serve with wedges of this hearty sandwich. Then serve the easy meal on colorful sturdy disposable plates.

Mediterranean Chicken Focaccia

Garlicky Turkey Burgers
Nacho Celery
Creamy Cole Slaw
Lemonade

4 servings

1 Make a can of frozen lemonade.

2 Heat the broiler. Shape and broil the turkey patties.

3 While the patties cook, fill celery with cheese mixture.

4 Mix a bag of coleslaw mix with purchased coleslaw dressing.

Nacho Celery

1 cup smoke-flavored cold-pack cheese food (from 8-oz. container)
1 teaspoon 40% less sodium taco seasoning mix (from 1.25-oz. package)
4 stalks (10 inch) celery
1/2 cup coarsely crushed French-fried onions (from 2.8-oz. can)

1 In small bowl, combine cheese food and taco seasoning mix; mix well.

2 Spread mixture in celery stalks. Top with onions. Cut into 2-inch pieces.

1 SERVING
Calories 240 (Calories from Fat 150);
Total Fat 17g (Saturated Fat 7g);
Cholesterol 40mg; Sodium 530mg;
Total Carbohydrates 11g (Dietary Fiber 1g);
Sugars 6g; Protein 11g
% Daily Value: Vitamin A 15%;
Vitamin C 4%; Calcium 30%; Iron 0%
Exchanges: 1⁄2 Starch, 1 1⁄2 High-Fat Meat, 1 Fat
Carbohydrate Choices: 1

QUICK FIX

These crunchy treats are perfect to make ahead and have on hand when it's time for dinner. Just store them in a tightly covered container in the refrigerator.

Garlicky Turkey Burgers

1 lb. lean ground turkey
1/2 cup refrigerated shredded
    hash brown potatoes
1/4 cup sliced green onions
2 tablespoons grated
    Parmesan cheese
2 teaspoons minced garlic
1/4 teaspoon seasoned salt
1/8 teaspoon pepper
1/4 cup mayonnaise or salad
    dressing, if desired
4 whole wheat hamburger buns, split
4 lettuce leaves
4 slices tomato, if desired

1 In medium bowl, combine all ingredients
except mayonnaise, buns and lettuce; mix well.
Shape into 4 (1/2-inch-thick) patties. Place patties on
broiler pan.

2 Broil 4 to 6 inches from heat for 8 to 10 minutes or
until thermometer inserted in center of patties reads 165°F.

3 Spread mayonnaise on cut sides of buns. Place lettuce, turkey
burgers and tomato on bottom halves of buns. Cover with
top halves of buns.

1 SERVING

Calories 300 (Calories from Fat 80); Total
Fat 9g (Saturated Fat 3g); Cholesterol 80mg;
Sodium 450mg; Total Carbohydrates 26g
(Dietary Fiber 4g); Sugars 3g; Protein 31g

% Daily Value: Vitamin A 2%;
Vitamin C 4%; Calcium 10%; Iron 15%

Exchanges: 1 1/2 Starch, 3 1/2 Very Lean
Meat, 1 Fat

Carbohydrate Choices: 2

QUICK FIX

It's easy to shape meat patties with a burger press available at kitchen specialty stores. This
handy gadget quickly forms patties of uniform thickness. If you don't have one, use a 1/2-cup
measuring cup for each patty, and press the meat with your fingers to the required thickness.

Family Heroes *Superfast*

4 sandwiches

1/4 cup Thousand Island salad dressing
4 hoagie buns, split
4 large lettuce leaves
3/4 lb. sliced cooked turkey
8 thin slices tomato (1 large)
1/4 lb. sliced hard salami
1 small cucumber, thinly sliced
4 slices American cheese, halved

1. Spread salad dressing evenly on cut sides of buns.
2. Layer bottom halves of buns with lettuce, turkey, tomato, salami, cucumber and cheese. Cover with top halves of buns.

1 SANDWICH

Calories 690 (Calories from Fat 280); Total Fat 31g (Saturated Fat 11g); Cholesterol 110mg; Sodium 1,610mg; Total Carbohydrates 57g (Dietary Fiber 4g); Sugars 7g; Protein 46g

% Daily Value: Vitamin A 15%; Vitamin C 20%; Calcium 25%; Iron 30%

Exchanges: 3 1/2 Starch, 5 Lean Meat, 2 1/2 Fat, 1/2 Other Carbohydrate

Carbohydrate Choices: 4

QUICK FIX

Is your family busy and off in different directions? These sandwiches are perfect to wrap individually in plastic wrap and have on hand in the refrigerator to grab and go. Store the sandwiches for up to 24 hours.

Family Heroes

Swiss Almond Turkey Sandwiches *Superfast*

■ ■ ■ ■ **Ready in 10 minutes**

4 sandwiches

1/2 cup Swiss almond cold-pack cheese food, softened
8 slices unfrosted raisin bread
4 small leaves leaf lettuce
1 lb. thinly sliced cooked turkey breast (from deli)
16 thin slices cucumber
4 radishes, thinly sliced

1 Spread 1 tablespoon cheese food on each bread slice. Top each of 4 slices evenly with lettuce, turkey, cucumber and radishes.

2 Cover sandwiches with remaining bread slices, cheese side down. Cut sandwiches in half diagonally.

1 SANDWICH

Calories 370 (Calories from Fat 120);
Total Fat 14g (Saturated Fat 7g);
Cholesterol 80mg; Sodium 1,990mg;
Total Carbohydrates 32g (Dietary
Fiber 3g); Sugars 13g; Protein 32g

% Daily Value: Vitamin A 10%;
Vitamin C 10%; Calcium 30%; Iron 15%

Exchanges: 2 Starch, 4 Very Lean Meat,
2 Fat

Carbohydrate Choices: 2

QUICK FIX

If you don't have Swiss almond cold-pack cheese food on hand, top each sandwich with a slice or two of cheese such as Swiss, American or Cheddar. You may want to spread each bread slice with butter or mayonnaise.

Fish Hero Sandwiches

■ ■ ■ ■ **Ready in 25 minutes**   *5 sandwiches*

5 frozen crisp battered fish fillets
1 can (10.2 oz.) large refrigerated buttermilk homestyle biscuits (5 biscuits)
1/2 cup sandwich spread, mayonnaise or salad dressing
1 1/4 cups shredded lettuce
5 slices Canadian bacon
5 slices American cheese
5 thin slices tomato

1 In 15 × 10-inch pan or on large cookie sheet, prepare fish fillets as directed on package, except during last 15 minutes of baking, reduce oven temperature to 375°F.

2 Remove fish from oven. Move fish to one side of pan. Separate dough into 5 biscuits; place 1 inch apart in same pan.

3 Return pan to oven; bake at 375°F for 11 to 15 minutes or until biscuits are golden brown and fish is thoroughly heated.

4 Split warm biscuits; spread each biscuit half with sandwich spread. Top bottom halves of biscuits with lettuce, Canadian bacon, fish fillet, cheese and tomato. Cover with top halves of biscuits.

1 SANDWICH

Calories 570 (Calories from Fat 300); Total Fat 33g (Saturated Fat 10g); Cholesterol 115mg; Sodium 1,870mg; Total Carbohydrates 44g (Dietary Fiber 1g); Sugars 6g; Protein 24g

% Daily Value: Vitamin A 10%; Vitamin C 2%; Calcium 20%; Iron 10%

Exchanges: 3 Starch, 2 Medium-Fat Meat, 4 Fat

Carbohydrate Choices: 3

QUICK FIX

Not in the mood to wash the pan? It won't be necessary if you line it with heavy-duty foil before baking the fish and biscuits.

Stand-Up Chicken Tacos
Southwestern-Style Corn Chowder
Strawberry-Banana Yogurt Smoothie   *5 servings*

Action Plan

1 Cook the chicken mixture for the tacos.

2 Heat 2 cans of ready-to-serve southwestern-style corn chowder.

3 While the soup heats, make the chicken tacos.

4 Make the smoothies.

Strawberry-Banana Yogurt Smoothie

3 cups fresh strawberries or individually frozen
   strawberries, slightly thawed
3 medium ripe bananas, cut up
1 1/2 cups milk
3 containers (8 oz.) low-fat strawberry yogurt

1 In blender container, place 1 1/2 cups strawberries, half of the banana pieces, 3/4 cup milk and 1 1/2 containers of yogurt. Cover; blend at medium speed 30 to 60 seconds or until smooth.

2 Repeat with remaining ingredients. Serve immediately.

1 SERVING

Calories 270 (Calories from Fat 30);
Total Fat 3.5g (Saturated Fat 2g);
Cholesterol 11mg; Sodium 120mg;
Total Carbohydrates 53g (Dietary Fiber 4g);
Sugars 34g; Protein 10g

% Daily Value: Vitamin A 6%;
Vitamin C 80%; Calcium 31%; Iron 4%

Exchanges: 2 Fruit, 1 Low-Fat Milk

Carbohydrate Choices: 4 1/2

QUICK FIX

For a mixed-berry smoothie, use another berry-flavored yogurt such as raspberry or cherry.

Stand-Up Chicken Tacos

1 package (4.7 oz.) taco shells that stand on their own
   (10 shells)
1 tablespoon vegetable oil
1 lb. chicken breast tenders, cut into 1-inch
   pieces
3 garlic cloves, minced
2 to 3 tablespoons taco seasoning mix (from
   1.25-oz. package)
2 tablespoons lime juice
2 cups mixed salad greens or shredded iceberg
   lettuce
1 medium tomato, chopped (3/4 cup)
1 cup shredded Cheddar cheese (4 oz.)
3/4 cup chunky-style salsa, if desired
2/3 cup sour cream, if desired

1. Heat oven to 325°F. Heat taco shells as directed on package.
2. Meanwhile, in 10-inch nonstick skillet, heat oil over medium-high heat until hot. Add chicken and garlic; cook and stir 2 to 4 minutes or until chicken is no longer pink in center.
3. Stir in taco seasoning mix and lime juice. Reduce heat to medium-low; cook 1 to 2 minutes or until thoroughly heated, stirring occasionally. Remove from heat.
4. Spoon chicken mixture into taco shells. Top each with salad greens, tomato and cheese. Serve tacos with salsa and sour cream.

1 SERVING
Calories 380 (Calories from Fat 170); Total Fat 19g (Saturated Fat 7g); Cholesterol 80mg; Sodium 500mg; Total Carbohydrates 23g (Dietary Fiber 3g); Sugars 3g; Protein 29g
% Daily Value: Vitamin A 30%; Vitamin C 10%; Calcium 20%; Iron 10%
Exchanges: 1 1/2 Starch, 3 1/2 Very Lean Meat, 3 Fat
Carbohydrate Choices: 1 1/2

QUICK FIX

Chicken tenders work great because they are 1-inch strips and you just need to cut them into pieces. If you don't have chicken tenders, use 4 boneless skinless chicken breasts instead.

Tuna Pita Sandwiches *Superfast*

■ ■ ■ ■ Ready in 10 minutes

6 sandwiches

1 can (6 oz.) tuna in water, drained, flaked
1 can (8 oz.) crushed pineapple, well drained
1/4 cup shredded carrot
3 tablespoons light mayonnaise
3 whole wheat or white pita breads (6 inch)
Leaf lettuce, if desired

1 In small bowl, combine tuna, pineapple, carrot and mayonnaise; mix well.

2 Cut pita breads in half crosswise; open each half to form pocket. Place lettuce and 1/4 cup tuna mixture in each pocket.

1 SANDWICH

Calories 160 (Calories from Fat 35); Total Fat 4g (Saturated Fat 1g); Cholesterol 10mg; Sodium 310mg; Total Carbohydrates 22g (Dietary Fiber 3g); Sugars 4g; Protein 9g

% Daily Value: Vitamin A 30%; Vitamin C 8%; Calcium 2%; Iron 10%

Exchanges: 1 1/2 Starch, 1/2 Very Lean Meat, 1/2 Fat

Carbohydrate Choices: 1 1/2

QUICK FIX Mix up the tuna mixture, then cover and store in the refrigerator for quick sandwiches anytime!

Tuna Pita Sandwiches

Cheesy Snackwiches

■ ■ ■ ■ Ready in 20 minutes

4 servings (2 snackwiches each)

1/2 cup shredded Cheddar cheese (2 oz.)
1/2 cup shredded Muenster cheese (2 oz.)
1/4 cup mayonnaise
1 jar (2 oz.) diced pimientos, drained
1/8 teaspoon onion powder
16 slices cocktail rye bread

1 In small bowl, combine all ingredients except bread; mix well.

2 Spread cheese mixture on 8 bread slices. Top with remaining bread slices.

1 SERVING

Calories 280 (Calories from Fat 190);
Total Fat 21g (Saturated Fat 8g);
Cholesterol 35mg; Sodium 440mg;
Total Carbohydrates 15g (Dietary
Fiber 2g); Sugars 2g; Protein 10g

% Daily Value: Vitamin A 14%;
Vitamin C 20%; Calcium 20%; Iron 6%

Exchanges: 1 Starch, 1 High-Fat Meat, 2 Fat

Carbohydrate Choices: 1

QUICK FIX

There's no need to ever shred cheese! Just look for a variety of shredded cheeses in the dairy department. If you want to use a different combination, go ahead and be creative. Why not try mozzarella and Parmesan or Monterey Jack and Colby?

If you have a block of knives, chances are there's a pair of scissors stuck in there, too. This oft-forgotten gadget can assist you in a variety of inventive ways.

1. Cut uncooked chicken breasts into small strips or cubes for stir-fries, soups or pastas.

2. Make quick (and clean) work of chopping up canned whole tomatoes by using kitchen scissors right in the opened can.

3. Effortlessly snip parsley, basil, chives and other herbs into tiny pieces.

4. Cut pizza or quesadillas into wedges.

5. Cut bacon, anchovies, sun-dried tomatoes and green onions into small pieces.

6. Trim the fat from poultry such as chicken or duck.

Nacho Bagels *Superfast*

■ ■ ■ ■ Ready in 15 minutes   *4 sandwiches*

2 bagels, split, toasted
4 thin slices tomato
4 oz. Mexican pasteurized prepared cheese product
    with jalapeño peppers, sliced
1/4 cup real bacon pieces

1. Top each toasted bagel half with tomato, cheese and bacon. Place on broiler pan or ungreased cookie sheet.
2. Broil 4 to 6 inches from heat for 1 to 2 minutes or until cheese is bubbly.

1 SANDWICH

Calories 200 (Calories from Fat 70); Total Fat 8g (Saturated Fat 5g); Cholesterol 25mg; Sodium 820mg; Total Carbohydrates 22g (Dietary Fiber 1g); Sugars 3g; Protein 11g

% Daily Value: Vitamin A 6%; Vitamin C 2%; Calcium 20%; Iron 8%

Exchanges: 1 1/2 Starch, 1 High-Fat Meat

Carbohydrate Choices: 1 1/2

QUICK FIX

Serve these quick open-faced sandwiches on colorful paper napkins. They're perfect to grab and go when you're in a hurry!

Garden Panini *Superfast*

Ready in 15 minutes

4 servings (2 wedges each)

1/2 cup cream cheese with garden vegetables
    (from 8-oz. container)
4 ready-to-serve Italian pizza crusts (6 inch)
2 cups fresh spinach leaves
8 thin slices tomato
1 medium yellow or orange bell pepper,
    cut into rings
16 thin slices cucumber

1. Spread cream cheese evenly on bottoms of each pizza crust.
2. On cream cheese side of 2 crusts, layer spinach, tomato, bell pepper and cucumber. Top with remaining pizza crusts, cream cheese side down. Cut each into 4 wedges.

1 SERVING

Calories 445 (Calories from Fat 160); Total Fat 18g (Saturated Fat 10g); Cholesterol 45mg; Sodium 690mg; Total Carbohydrates 55g (Dietary Fiber 3g); Sugars 4g; Protein 16g

% Daily Value: Vitamin A 48%; Vitamin C 100%; Calcium 6%; Iron 24%

Exchanges: 3 Starch, 1 Vegetable, 1/2 High-Fat Meat, 2 1/2 Fat

Carbohydrate Choices: 3 1/2

QUICK FIX

For ultra-convenience, look for packages of washed baby spinach leaves where you find bags of mixed greens. You won't miss the stems or washing the leaves.

Bean and Veggie Burgers

4 sandwiches

1 can (15 or 15.5 oz.) kidney beans, rinsed and drained
1/2 cup uncooked oats
1/2 cup chopped fresh mushrooms
1/4 cup chopped onion
1 small carrot, shredded (1/2 cup)
1/2 medium red bell pepper, chopped (1/2 cup)
1 garlic clove, minced
2 tablespoons ketchup
3/4 teaspoon salt
4 lettuce leaves
4 slices tomato
4 burger buns, split
Ketchup or mustard, if desired

1. Spray broiler pan rack with cooking spray. In food processor bowl with metal blade, combine beans, oats, mushrooms, onion, carrot, bell pepper, garlic, ketchup and salt; process with on/off pulses until coarsely chopped. DO NOT PUREE.
2. Shape mixture into 4 (1/2-inch-thick) patties. Place patties on broiler pan.
3. Broil 4 to 6 inches from heat for 10 to 12 minutes or until patties are thoroughly heated, turning once.
4. Place lettuce, tomato and patties on bottom halves of buns. Top with ketchup or mustard. Cover with top halves of buns.

1 SANDWICH

Calories 270 (Calories from Fat 25); Total Fat 3g (Saturated Fat 1g); Cholesterol 0mg; Sodium 860mg; Total Carbohydrates 49g (Dietary Fiber 7g); Sugars 9g; Protein 11g

% Daily Value: Vitamin A 90%; Vitamin C 25%; Calcium 10%; Iron 20%

Exchanges: 2 1/2 Starch, 1/2 Very Lean Meat, 1/2 Fat, 1/2 Other Carbohydrate

Carbohydrate Choices: 3

QUICK FIX

Cleanup is a snap when you cover the broiler pan rack with foil before spraying with the cooking spray. Use a knife to make small slits in the foil so any juices can drip through to the pan underneath. Then just toss the foil when you're done!

Bean and Veggie Burgers

Taco Cheese Quesadillas Superfast

Ready in 10 minutes

4 flour tortillas (8 to 9 inch)
2 cups shredded taco-flavored cheese blend (8 oz.)
4 Italian plum tomatoes, thinly sliced
2 tablespoons chopped fresh cilantro, if desired
4 teaspoons oil

1. Place 2 tortillas on ungreased cookie sheet. Sprinkle each tortilla with 3/4 cup of the cheese. Arrange tomatoes over cheese; sprinkle with cilantro. Top with remaining tortillas.
2. Brush tops of quesadillas with 2 teaspoons of the oil. Broil 4 to 6 inches from heat for 1 to 2 minutes.
3. Remove from broiler. With 2 large pancake turners, carefully turn quesadillas over. Brush with remaining 2 teaspoons oil. Sprinkle tops with remaining 1/2 cup cheese.
4. Return to broiler; broil an additional 1 to 2 minutes or until cheese is melted and quesadillas are light golden brown. Cut each into 6 wedges.

1 SERVING

Calories 275 (Calories from Fat 155); Total Fat 17g (Saturated Fat 8g); Cholesterol 35mg; Sodium 380mg; Total Carbohydrates 18g (Dietary Fiber 1g); Sugars 2g; Protein 12g

% Daily Value: Vitamin A 14%; Vitamin C 6%; Calcium 30%; Iron 6%

Exchanges: 1 Starch, 1 1/2 High-Fat Meat, 1 Fat

Carbohydrate Choices: 1

QUICK FIX

Pick up a bag of mixed greens in the produce department, then add your favorite salad dressing and toss a salad right in the bag to serve with these easy quesadillas.

Tropical Peanut Butter Burritos *Superfast*

■ ■ ■ ■ Ready in 15 minutes

4 burritos

4 tablespoons peanut butter
4 flour tortillas (8 inch)
4 tablespoons drained crushed pineapple in unsweetened juice
1 large banana, thinly sliced
4 tablespoons coconut

1 Spread about 1 tablespoon peanut butter on each tortilla. Top each with 1 tablespoon pineapple, 1/4 of the banana slices and 1 tablespoon coconut.

2 Roll up each tortilla. Serve immediately.

1 BURRITO

Calories 280 (Calories from Fat 110); Total Fat 12g (Saturated Fat 4g); Cholesterol 0mg; Sodium 250mg; Total Carbohydrates 35g (Dietary Fiber 3g); Sugars 10g; Protein 8g

% Daily Value: Vitamin A 0%; Vitamin C 8%; Calcium 6%; Iron 10%

Exchanges: 1 1/2 Starch, 1 Fruit, 1/2 High-Fat Meat, 1 Fat

Carbohydrate Choices: 2

QUICK FIX

Store the remaining pineapple in a tightly covered container in the refrigerator for a fruity snack later.

Two

Quick from the Stovetop

Superfast Ready in 15 minutes or less

Hamburger Divan Skillet

6 servings (1 1/2 cups each)

6 oz. uncooked spaghetti, broken into 2-inch pieces (1 1/2 cups)
3 cups frozen cut broccoli (from 1-lb. bag)
1 1/2 lb. lean (at least 80%) ground beef
1 container (10 oz.) refrigerated Alfredo pasta sauce
1/3 cup half-and-half
1 package (3 oz.) cream cheese, cut into cubes
1 jar (6 oz.) sliced mushrooms, drained
1 cup shredded Cheddar cheese (4 oz.)

1 Cook spaghetti as directed on package, adding broccoli during last minute of cooking time. Drain; return to saucepan. Cover to keep warm.

2 Meanwhile, in 10-inch skillet, cook ground beef over medium-high heat for 5 to 7 minutes or until thoroughly cooked, stirring frequently. Drain. Reduce heat to medium.

3 Stir in pasta sauce, half-and-half, cream cheese and mushrooms. Cook an additional 2 to 3 minutes or until cream cheese is melted and mixture is thoroughly heated, stirring frequently.

4 Stir in cooked spaghetti and broccoli; cook an additional minute until broccoli is hot. Sprinkle with Cheddar cheese.

1 SERVING

Calories 675 (Calories from Fat 405); Total Fat 45g (Saturated Fat 24g); Cholesterol 150mg; Sodium 660mg; Total Carbohydrates 31g (Dietary Fiber 3g); Sugars 4g; Protein 37g

% Daily Value: Vitamin A 38%; Vitamin C 16%; Calcium 28%; Iron 22%

Exchanges: 2 Starch, 1 Vegetable, 4 Medium-Fat Meat, 5 Fat

Carbohydrate Choices: 2

QUICK FIX

For a change, try 1 1/2 pounds bulk Italian sausage instead of the ground beef. Use mild sausage, or for a little more zip, use hot sausage.

Hamburger Hash Skillet Supper

■ ■ ■ ■ **Ready in 25 minutes**

5 servings (1 1/3 cups each)

1 lb. lean (at least 80%) ground beef
1 bag (1 lb. 4 oz.) refrigerated diced potatoes with onions
1/2 cup chopped red onion
1/3 cup whipping cream
1 tablespoon Worcestershire sauce
1 teaspoon celery salt
1/4 teaspoon pepper
2 medium tomatoes, chopped (1 1/4 cups)

1 In 12-inch nonstick skillet, cook ground beef, potatoes and red onion over medium heat for 10 to 15 minutes or until beef is thoroughly cooked and potatoes are tender, stirring frequently. Drain well.

2 Stir cream, Worcestershire sauce, celery salt and pepper into beef mixture; blend well. Cook an additional 2 to 5 minutes or until mixture is bubbly around edges, stirring frequently. Gently stir in tomatoes.

1 SERVING

Calories 350 (Calories from Fat 160);
Total Fat 18g (Saturated Fat 8g);
Cholesterol 70mg; Sodium 660mg;
Total Carbohydrates 27g
(Dietary Fiber 2g); Sugars 4g; Protein 20g

% Daily Value: Vitamin A 12%;
Vitamin C 14%; Calcium 4%; Iron 12%

Exchanges: 2 Starch, 2 Medium-Fat Meat,
1 1/2 Fat

Carbohydrate Choices: 2

QUICK FIX

Thaw frozen ground beef quickly in the microwave on Defrost for 4 to 6 minutes. If necessary, microwave in additional increments of 30 seconds until thawed. It helps to turn the package over once or twice while it is thawing.

Hamburger Hash Skillet Supper

Hamburger and Potato Skillet

■ ■ ■ ■ Ready in 25 minutes

4 servings (1 3/4 cups each)

3 cups frozen mini potato nuggets (from 28-oz. bag)
1 lb. lean (at least 80%) ground beef
2 garlic cloves, minced or 1/4 teaspoon garlic powder
2 cups frozen cut green beans (from 1-lb. bag)
1/4 cup milk
1 can (10.75 oz.) condensed cream of celery soup
1 cup shredded American cheese (4 oz.)

1. Cook potato nuggets as directed on package.
2. Meanwhile, in 10-inch skillet, cook ground beef and garlic over medium-high heat for 5 to 7 minutes or until thoroughly cooked, stirring frequently. Drain. Add beans, milk and soup; mix well. Reduce heat to medium; cook 6 to 8 minutes or until beans are tender, stirring occasionally.
3. Add cheese; stir until melted. Top with cooked potato nuggets.

1 SERVING

Calories 620 (Calories from Fat 330); Total Fat 37g (Saturated Fat 17g); Cholesterol 105mg; Sodium 1,750mg; Total Carbohydrates 39g (Dietary Fiber 5g); Sugars 5g; Protein 32g

% Daily Value: Vitamin A 15%; Vitamin C 15%; Calcium 25%; Iron 25%

Exchanges: 2 Starch, 1 Vegetable, 3 1/2 Medium–Fat Meat, 3 1/2 Fat, 1/2 Other Carbohydrate

Carbohydrate Choices: 2

QUICK FIX

For easy cleanup all the time, invest in a good-quality nonstick skillet. Pans with a hard anodized surface are the most durable, will last the longest and provide the most even cooking.

Skillet Spanish Beef 'n Rice

■ ■ ■ ■ **Ready in 20 minutes**　　　　　　　　　*4 servings (1 1/2 cups each)*

3/4 lb. extra-lean (at least 90%) ground beef
1/2 medium green bell pepper, chopped (1/2 cup)
1 medium zucchini, quartered lengthwise, sliced (2 cups)
1 can (8 oz.) tomato sauce
1 cup water
1/2 teaspoon salt
1/2 teaspoon dried oregano leaves
1/2 teaspoon chili powder
1 1/2 cups uncooked instant white rice

1 In 10-inch nonstick skillet, cook ground beef over medium-high heat for 5 to 7 minutes or until thoroughly cooked, stirring frequently. Drain.

2 Stir in bell pepper, zucchini, tomato sauce, water, salt, oregano and chili powder. Bring to a boil. Cover; cook over low heat for 2 to 3 minutes or until vegetables are tender.

3 Stir in rice. Cover; cook over low heat for 5 to 8 minutes or until liquid is absorbed. Fluff with fork before serving.

1 SERVING
Calories 320 (Calories from Fat 100);
Total Fat 11g (Saturated Fat 4g);
Cholesterol 55mg; Sodium 660mg;
Total Carbohydrates 36g (Dietary Fiber 2g);
Sugars 4g; Protein 20g

% Daily Value: Vitamin A 20%;
Vitamin C 25%; Calcium 2%; Iron 20%

Exchanges: 2 Starch, 1 Vegetable,
2 Medium-Fat Meat

Carbohydrate Choices: 2 1/2

QUICK FIX

Don't peel unless you have to! With some vegetables such as zucchini and other summer squash, it's fine—and faster—to simply wash the skins before slicing.

Veggie Salisbury Steak

4 servings

4 (4-oz.) ground beef patties
1/2 teaspoon peppered seasoned salt
1 cup frozen mixed vegetables (from 1-lb. bag)
1 medium onion, chopped (1/2 cup)
2 tablespoons ketchup
1 tablespoon Worcestershire sauce
1 jar (4.5 oz.) sliced mushrooms, drained
1 jar (12 oz.) beef gravy

1 Heat 12-inch nonstick skillet over medium-high heat until hot. Add beef patties; sprinkle with peppered seasoned salt. Cook 3 to 5 minutes or until brown on both sides, turning once.

2 In medium bowl, combine all remaining ingredients; mix well. Add to skillet; bring to a boil. Reduce heat to medium-low; cover and simmer 10 to 12 minutes or until meat thermometer inserted in center of patties reads 160°F and vegetables are tender, stirring and turning patties once or twice.

1 SERVING

Calories 340 (Calories from Fat 180); Total Fat 20g (Saturated Fat 8g); Cholesterol 70mg; Sodium 990mg; Total Carbohydrates 16g (Dietary Fiber 3g); Sugars 6g; Protein 24g

% Daily Value: Vitamin A 44%; Vitamin C 6%; Calcium 4%; Iron 18%

Exchanges: 1 Starch, 3 Medium-Fat Meat, 1 Fat

Carbohydrate Choices: 1

QUICK FIX

Chopping not on your schedule? Look for frozen chopped onion in packages where you find frozen vegetables. Measure the quantity that you need, and wrap the remainder tightly for the next time a recipe requires chopped onion.

Veggie Salisbury Steak

Baby Carrots with Ranch Dressing Dip
Chili-Cheese Hash Browns
Banana Roll-Ups

4 servings

1. Heat the chili and cook the hash-brown potato patties.
2. While the chili and potatoes cook, make the banana roll-ups but leave whole. Cover with plastic wrap and refrigerate.
3. Spoon the ranch dressing into individual bowls. Serve with raw baby carrots for dipping. Make the chili-cheese hash browns.
4. For dessert, cut roll-ups into 1-inch pieces. Top with ice cream, topping and whipped cream.

Banana Roll-Ups

3 tablespoons peanut butter
2 flour tortillas (7- to 8- inch)
2 tablespoons hot fudge ice cream topping
2 bananas
2 teaspoons toasted wheat germ, if desired
1 pint (2 cups) chocolate or vanilla ice cream
Additional hot fudge ice cream topping, if desired

1. Spread peanut butter on tortillas. Carefully spread ice cream topping over peanut butter.
2. Place banana in center of each tortilla. (If bananas are very curved, make 2 cuts at intervals on inside edge to make them lay straight.) Sprinkle each with wheat germ. Roll up tortillas; cut each into 1-inch pieces.
3. Arrange roll-ups on 4 dessert plates; top each with cup ice cream and ice cream topping.

1 SERVING

Calories 350 (Calories from Fat 140); Total Fat 16g (Saturated Fat 7g); Cholesterol 30mg; Sodium 220mg; Total Carbohydrates 47g (Dietary Fiber 3g); Sugars 25g; Protein 8g

% Daily Value: Vitamin A 6%; Vitamin C 10%; Calcium 10%; Iron 6%

Exchanges: 2 Starch, 1 Fruit, 3 Fat

Carbohydrate Choices: 3

QUICK FIX
For a peanut butter and "jelly" roll-up, use strawberry ice cream topping instead of chocolate. Kids of all ages will love this easy dessert.

Chili-Cheese Hash Browns

1 package (12 oz.) frozen chili or
  15-oz. can chili
4 frozen rectangular hash-brown
  potato patties (from 27-oz. box)
Oil for frying
1/2 cup finely shredded Cheddar cheese
  (2 oz.)
1/2 cup chunky-style salsa
1 tablespoon chopped fresh cilantro, if
  desired

1 Heat chili as directed on package or can.
  Fry potato patties in oil as directed on package.

2 To serve, place potato patties on individual serving plates.
  Top each serving with chili. Sprinkle each with cheese.
  Top with salsa and cilantro.

QUICK FIX

Stop at the deli and pick up some creamy coleslaw to complete this easy meal. Save on dishes by serving the coleslaw right from the deli container.

1 SERVING

Calories 340 (Calories from Fat 200);
Total Fat 22g (Saturated Fat 6g);
Cholesterol 30mg; Sodium 600mg;
Total Carbohydrates 25g (Dietary
Fiber 4g); Sugars 4g; Protein 11g
% Daily Value: Vitamin A 15%;
Vitamin C 15%; Calcium 15%; Iron 6%
Exchanges: 1 1/2 Starch, 1 Medium-Fat
Meat, 3 Fat
Carbohydrate Choices: 1 1/2

Taco-Topped Potatoes

4 servings

4 medium baking potatoes
1 container (18 oz.) refrigerated taco sauce with seasoned ground beef
1/2 cup shredded Cheddar cheese (2 oz.)
1 medium Italian plum tomato, chopped (1/3 cup)
2 medium green onions, sliced (2 tablespoons)

1 Pierce potatoes with fork. Arrange in spoke pattern on microwave-safe paper towel in microwave. Microwave on High for 12 to 14 minutes or until tender, turning potatoes and rearranging halfway through cooking. Cool 3 minutes.

2 Meanwhile, heat taco sauce with seasoned ground beef as directed on container.

3 To serve, place potatoes on individual serving plates. Cut potatoes in half lengthwise; mash slightly with fork. Spoon about 1/2 cup ground beef mixture over each potato. Top with cheese, tomato and onions.

1 SERVING

Calories 340 (Calories from Fat 155); Total Fat 17g (Saturated Fat 8g); Cholesterol 50mg; Sodium 770mg; Total Carbohydrates 35g (Dietary Fiber 2g); Sugars 7g; Protein 21g

% Daily Value: Vitamin A 6%; Vitamin C 12%; Calcium 8%; Iron 2%

Exchanges: 2 Starch, 1 Vegetable, 2 Medium-Fat Meat

Carbohydrate Choices: 2

QUICK FIX

Look for tubs of the taco sauce with seasoned ground beef in the refrigerated meat case at the grocery store. It's a great product to have on hand for quick tacos or meals such as this. The microwavable ground beef is ready to serve in 6 minutes and can be frozen for longer storage.

Taco-Topped Potatoes

Mexican Beef Skillet Dinner

■ ■ ■ ■ ■ **Ready in 20 minutes**   *5 servings (1 1/2 cups each)*

1 lb. lean (at least 80%) ground beef
1 small onion, chopped (1/3 cup)
1 garlic clove, minced or 1/8 teaspoon garlic powder
1 can (10.75 oz.) condensed cream of mushroom soup
1 can (4.5 oz.) chopped green chiles
1 can (10 oz.) enchilada sauce
2 cups tortilla chips, broken slightly
1 cup shredded Cheddar cheese (4 oz.)
2 tablespoons chopped fresh cilantro, if desired

1. In 10-inch skillet, cook ground beef, onion and garlic over medium-high heat for 5 to 7 minutes or until beef is thoroughly cooked, stirring frequently. Drain.

2. Stir in soup, chiles, enchilada sauce and chips. Reduce heat to medium; cook and stir 3 to 4 minutes or until thoroughly heated and bubbly.

3. Sprinkle with cheese. Cover; cook an additional 2 to 3 minutes or until cheese is melted. Sprinkle with cilantro.

1 SERVING

Calories 480 (Calories from Fat 280); Total Fat 31g (Saturated Fat 12g); Cholesterol 80mg; Sodium 1,030mg; Total Carbohydrates 24g (Dietary Fiber 3g); Sugars 4g; Protein 25g

% Daily Value: Vitamin A 15%; Vitamin C 10%; Calcium 25%; Iron 15%

Exchanges: 1 1/2 Starch, 3 Medium-Fat Meat, 3 Fat

Carbohydrate Choices: 1 1/2

QUICK FIX

Look for chopped garlic in jars in the produce area of the grocery store. It's a great time-saving product; just follow the label directions for amounts to use.

Breaded Honey Mustard Pork

4 servings

2 tablespoons honey mustard
1 egg
1/2 cup unseasoned dry bread crumbs
1/2 teaspoon garlic-pepper blend
1/4 teaspoon salt
1 lb. pork tenderloin, cut crosswise into 8 pieces
1 to 2 tablespoons vegetable oil

1 In shallow bowl, combine mustard and egg; beat well. In another shallow bowl, combine bread crumbs, garlic-pepper blend and salt; mix well.

2 To flatten each pork piece, place between 2 pieces of plastic wrap or waxed paper. Working from center, gently pound pork with flat side of meat mallet or rolling pin until about 1/4 inch thick; remove wrap.

3 Heat oil in 10-inch nonstick skillet over medium-high heat until hot. Coat each pork piece with mustard mixture, then crumbs; place in skillet. Cook 6 to 8 minutes or until brown on both sides and slightly pink in center, turning once.

1 SERVING

Calories 280 (Calories from Fat 120); Total Fat 13g (Saturated Fat 3g); Cholesterol 120mg; Sodium 440mg; Total Carbohydrates 13g (Dietary Fiber 1g); Sugars 2g; Protein 27g

% Daily Value: Vitamin A 0%; Vitamin C 0%; Calcium 4%; Iron 15%

Exchanges: 1 Starch, 3 1/2 Lean Meat, 1/2 Fat

Carbohydrate Choices: 1

QUICK FIX

For super-easy cleanup, use disposable foil pans or paper plates with a rim for the pork chop coatings, then just toss when you're done with the prep.

Zesty Skillet Pork Chops

■ ■ ■ ■ Ready in 20 minutes

4 servings

4 (3/4-inch-thick) boneless pork loin chops (1 1/4 lb.)
1/2 teaspoon garlic-pepper blend
1/4 teaspoon salt
3/4 cup barbecue sauce
1/2 cup chunky-style salsa

1 Heat 10-inch nonstick skillet over medium-high heat until hot. Sprinkle both sides of pork chops with garlic-pepper blend and salt; add to hot skillet. Cook 2 to 3 minutes or until brown on both sides.

2 Add barbecue sauce and salsa; turn to coat chops. Reduce heat to low; cover and simmer 10 to 15 minutes or until chops are slightly pink in center, turning chops and stirring sauce once or twice. Serve pork chops with sauce.

1 SERVING

Calories 295 (Calories from Fat 100); Total Fat 11g (Saturated Fat 4g); Cholesterol 85mg; Sodium 810mg; Total Carbohydrates 19g (Dietary Fiber 1g); Sugars 14g; Protein 31g

% Daily Value: Vitamin A 6%; Vitamin C 6%; Calcium 2%; Iron 10%

Exchanges: 1 Starch, 4 Lean Meat

Carbohydrate Choices: 1

QUICK FIX

Look for bargain prices on large packages of boneless pork chops, then wrap each pork chop individually in plastic wrap for freezer storage. Thaw the chops quickly in the microwave on nights when you require a quick meal like this.

Paper towels are the unsung heroes of the kitchen. From wiping windows to cleaning up countertops, their usefulness is virtually without limit.

1. Frying food is messy—even with a spatter screen. A paper towel placed on top of the spatter screen will absorb any grease and moisture coming off frying food and make cleanup a breeze.

2. Put several paper towels inside a plastic grocery bag (make sure the bag has no holes). Pop your rinsed lettuce in the bag, and swing the bag around. Ta da! Instant salad spinner (or would that be salad swinger?).

3. Strawberries will stay fresh longer when you put them—unwashed—into a bowl lined with a paper towel. Store the bowl, covered with another paper towel, in the refrigerator.

4. Keep a chunk of cheese fresh longer by wrapping it in a paper towel dipped in white vinegar (wring it out first). Store the cheese in a sealed plastic bag.

5. Slightly dampen a paper towel, then place it under your cutting board to prevent the board from slipping or skidding.

Chicken Fried Pork Chops
Mixed Vegetables
Mashed Potatoes
Red Grapefruit Tossed Salad

4 servings

1. Flatten, coat and cook the pork chops.
2. While pork chops cook, cook the mixed vegetables in the microwave.
3. Make the tossed salad.
4. Heat purchased refrigerated mashed potatoes in the microwave.

Red Grapefruit Tossed Salad

Dressing
1/4 cup sour cream
2 tablespoons frozen grapefruit juice concentrate, thawed
1 tablespoon brown sugar

Salad
3 cups mixed salad greens
1 large red, pink or white grapefruit, peeled, sectioned
1/4 large sweet onion, thinly sliced, separated into rings
    (Walla Walla, Maui or Texas Sweet)

1. In medium bowl, combine all dressing ingredients; blend well.
2. Add all salad ingredients; toss gently.

1 SERVING
Calories 90 (Calories from Fat 25);
Total Fat 3g (Saturated Fat 2g);
Cholesterol 10mg; Sodium 20mg;
Total Carbohydrates 15g (Dietary Fiber 2g);
Sugars 12g; Protein 2g
% Daily Value: Vitamin A 45%;
Vitamin C 80%; Calcium 6%; Iron 4%
Exchanges: 1/2 Fruit, 1 Vegetable, 1/2 Fat
Carbohydrate Choices: 1

QUICK FIX

Keep a jar of peeled, sectioned grapefruit on hand. You will find it in the produce refrigerator section. Use about half a jar of well-drained sections for this recipe when there just isn't time to peel and section a grapefruit.

Chicken Fried Pork Chops

4 (4-oz.) boneless pork loin chops
1/4 cup all-purpose flour
1/2 teaspoon seasoned salt
1/4 teaspoon garlic powder
2 to 3 tablespoons milk
1/2 cup Italian-style dry bread crumbs
2 tablespoons vegetable oil

1 To flatten each pork chop, place between 2 pieces of plastic wrap or waxed paper. Working from center, gently pound pork with flat side of meat mallet or rolling pin until about 1/4 inch thick; remove wrap.

2 In shallow bowl, combine flour, seasoned salt and garlic powder; mix well. Place milk and bread crumbs in separate shallow bowls. Dip each pork chop in flour mixture; dip in milk. Coat well with bread crumbs.

3 Heat oil in 10-inch skillet over medium heat until hot. Add pork chops; cook 6 to 8 minutes or until slightly pink in center.

1 SERVING

Calories 300 (Calories from Fat 140); Total Fat 15g (Saturated Fat 4g); Cholesterol 60mg; Sodium 450mg; Total Carbohydrates 17g (Dietary Fiber 1g); Sugars 1g; Protein 24g
% Daily Value: Vitamin A 0%; Vitamin C 0%; Calcium 4%; Iron 10%
Exchanges: 1 Starch, 3 Very Lean Meat, 2 1/2 Fat
Carbohydrate Choices: 1

QUICK FIX

Save on cleanup by using separate plastic bags for the seasoned flour and the bread crumbs, but leave the milk in the bowl. Just shake the pork chops in each bag to coat as directed in the recipe.

Supper Ham Frittata

■ ■ ■ ■ **Ready in 20 minutes**

4 servings

1 1/2 cups frozen southern-style cubed hash-brown
    potatoes (from 32-oz. bag)
1 small zucchini, quartered lengthwise, sliced (1 cup)
1 1/2 cups diced cooked ham
4 eggs
1/4 cup milk
1/4 teaspoon salt
1 cup shredded Cheddar cheese (4 oz.)

1 Heat 10-inch nonstick skillet over medium-high heat until hot. Add potatoes, zucchini and ham; cook 5 to 8 minutes or until zucchini is crisp-tender and potatoes are thoroughly cooked, stirring frequently.

2 Meanwhile, in medium bowl, beat eggs. Add milk and salt; beat well.

3 Pour egg mixture over mixture in skillet. Reduce heat to medium-low; cover and cook 5 to 7 minutes or until center is set, lifting edges occasionally to allow uncooked egg mixture to flow to bottom of skillet.

4 Sprinkle frittata with cheese. Cover; cook an additional 2 to 3 minutes or until cheese is melted. To serve, cut into wedges.

1 SERVING

Calories 360 (Calories from Fat 180); **Total Fat** 20g (Saturated Fat 9g); **Cholesterol** 275mg; **Sodium** 1,170mg; **Total Carbohydrates** 18g (Dietary Fiber 1g); Sugars 3g; Protein 27g

% Daily Value: Vitamin A 16%; Vitamin C 6%; Calcium 20%; Iron 10%

Exchanges: 1 Starch, 3 1/2 Medium-Fat Meat, 1/2 Fat

Carbohydrate Choices: 1

QUICK FIX

There's no need to spend time dicing ham—just look for handy packages of diced cooked ham near the packaged luncheon meats at the grocery store.

Biscuits with Pork Sausage Gravy

■ ■ ■ ■ Ready in 20 minutes

5 servings

1 can (12 oz.) refrigerated flaky or buttermilk flaky biscuits
1 lb. bulk pork sausage
1/4 cup butter
1/3 cup all-purpose flour
1/4 teaspoon garlic powder
1/4 teaspoon coarse ground black pepper
1 can (14 oz.) fat-free chicken broth with 1/3 less sodium
1/4 cup half-and-half

1. Bake biscuits as directed on can.
2. Meanwhile, crumble sausage into 10-inch skillet; cook over medium-high heat until brown and no longer pink, stirring frequently. Remove sausage from skillet. Drain. Set aside.
3. In 2-quart saucepan, melt butter over medium heat. With wire whisk, stir in flour, garlic powder and pepper; cook, stirring constantly, until mixture is smooth and bubbly. Gradually stir in broth and half-and-half. Bring to a boil; boil and stir 1 minute until mixture thickens. Stir in cooked sausage.
4. Split warm biscuits; place on individual serving plates. Spoon sausage mixture over biscuit halves.

1 SERVING
Calories 530 (Calories from Fat 305);
Total Fat 34g (Saturated Fat 14g);
Cholesterol 65mg; Sodium 1,610mg;
Total Carbohydrates 40g (Dietary
Fiber 1g); Sugars 11g; Protein 16g

% Daily Value: Vitamin A 8%;
Vitamin C 0%; Calcium 4%; Iron 16%

Exchanges: 2 1/2 Starch, 1 High-Fat Meat,
5 Fat

Carbohydrate Choices: 2 1/2

QUICK FIX

Refrigerated dough products, such as the biscuits used in this recipe, streamline prep for all kinds of dishes from side dishes to desserts. For the best results, remember that opening the can activates the leavening, so bake the dough as quickly as possible after opening it.

Sausage and Potato Skillet Sizzle

■ ■ ■ ■ Ready in 25 minutes

4 servings

1 tablespoon butter or margarine
1 cup frozen bell pepper and onion stir-fry (from 1-lb. bag)
1 bag (1 lb. 4 oz.) refrigerated new potato wedges
1/4 teaspoon pepper
6 oz. cooked, smoked turkey kielbasa or Polish sausage,
    cut into 1/4-inch slices
1 1/2 cups frozen broccoli florets (from 14-oz. bag)
1 1/2 cups frozen cauliflower florets (from 1-lb. bag)
1/2 cup shredded Cheddar and American cheese blend (2 oz.)

1 In 10-inch nonstick skillet, melt butter over medium heat. Add bell pepper and onion stir-fry, potatoes and pepper; cook 10 minutes, stirring occasionally.

2 Add kielbasa, broccoli and cauliflower; mix well. Cover; cook 8 to 10 minutes or until vegetables are tender, stirring occasionally. Remove from heat. Sprinkle with cheese; cover and let stand 1 to 2 minutes or until cheese is melted.

1 SERVING

Calories 290 (Calories from Fat 110); Total Fat 12g (Saturated Fat 6g); Cholesterol 45mg; Sodium 960mg; Total Carbohydrates 32g (Dietary Fiber 6g); Sugars 3g; Protein 14g

% Daily Value: Vitamin A 20%; Vitamin C 50%; Calcium 14%; Iron 18%

Exchanges: 1 1/2 Starch, 1 Vegetable, 1 Medium-Fat Meat, 1 1/2 Fat

Carbohydrate Choices: 2

QUICK FIX

Serve the finished meal right from the skillet. Just place it on a hot pad in the center of the table and add a serving spoon. There will be no serving dish to wash!

Sausage and Potato Skillet Sizzle

Home-Style Chicken and Gravy

■ ■ ■ ■ Ready in 25 minutes

6 servings

6 boneless skinless chicken breast halves
1/2 teaspoon seasoned salt
3/4 teaspoon paprika
3/4 teaspoon garlic-pepper blend
1 jar (12 oz.) chicken gravy
2 tablespoons fat-free half-and-half or milk
1 tablespoon Worcestershire sauce

1. Heat 10-inch nonstick skillet over medium-high heat until hot. Sprinkle chicken with seasoned salt, paprika and garlic-pepper blend; add to skillet. Cook 4 to 6 minutes or until brown on both sides.

2. In medium bowl, combine gravy, half-and-half and Worcestershire sauce; mix well. Pour gravy mixture over chicken. Cover; simmer over medium-low heat for 10 to 15 minutes or until juice of chicken is no longer pink when center of thickest part is cut.

1 SERVING
Calories 180 (Calories from Fat 50);
Total Fat 6g (Saturated Fat 2g);
Cholesterol 75mg; Sodium 580mg;
Total Carbohydrates 4g (Dietary Fiber 0g);
Sugars 0g; Protein 28g

% Daily Value: Vitamin A 8%;
Vitamin C 0%; Calcium 4%; Iron 6%

Exchanges: 1/2 Starch, 4 Very Lean Meat, 1/2 Fat

Carbohydrate Choices: 0

QUICK FIX

Don't have boneless chicken breasts on hand? Bone-in chicken breast halves can be used instead. Just simmer the chicken in the gravy mixture for 5 to 10 minutes longer than the recipe recommends.

Chicken Con Queso

■ ■ ■ ■ **Ready in 20 minutes**   *4 servings*

4 frozen breaded cooked chicken patties
2 cups uncooked instant white rice
2 cups water
1 1/2 cups chunky-style salsa
2 cups shredded American cheese (8 oz.)

1. Cook chicken patties as directed on package.
2. Meanwhile, cook rice in water as directed on package. Stir 1/2 cup of the salsa into rice. Cover to keep warm.
3. In 1 1/2-quart saucepan, combine remaining 1 cup salsa and the cheese; cook over low heat until cheese is melted, stirring occasionally.
4. Place cooked rice on individual serving plates. Top each serving with warm chicken patty. Spoon cheese sauce over top.

1 SERVING

Calories 620 (Calories from Fat 280); Total Fat 31g (Saturated Fat 14g); Cholesterol 85mg; Sodium 1,510mg; Total Carbohydrates 58g (Dietary Fiber 4g); Sugars 6g; Protein 27g

% Daily Value: Vitamin A 20%; Vitamin C 0%; Calcium 40%; Iron 15%

Exchanges: 4 Starch, 2 High-Fat Meat, 2 1/2 Fat

Carbohydrate Choices: 4

QUICK FIX

Use finely shredded cheese for this dish. It melts the fastest! And for a little added color and flavor, sprinkle with sliced green onions or olives.

Chicken, Mushroom and Asparagus Stir-Fry

■ ■ ■ ■ **Ready in 20 minutes**   *4 servings*

1 cup uncooked instant white rice
1 cup water
2 tablespoons vegetable oil
1 lb. chicken breast strips for stir-frying
1 lb. fresh asparagus spears, trimmed, cut into 2-inch pieces
1 medium onion, cut into 1/2-inch wedges
1 package (8 oz.) sliced fresh mushrooms (3 cups)
1/4 cup water
1/2 cup stir-fry sauce
1/4 cup oyster sauce

1. Cook rice in 1 cup water as directed on package.
2. Meanwhile, heat 1 tablespoon of the oil in wok or 10-inch skillet over medium-high heat until hot. Add chicken strips; cook and stir 5 to 6 minutes or until no longer pink in center. Remove chicken from wok; place on plate.
3. Add remaining tablespoon oil to wok. Add asparagus and onion; cook and stir 3 minutes. Add mushrooms; cook and stir an additional 3 minutes.
4. Add reserved chicken, 1/4 cup water, the stir-fry sauce and oyster sauce; cover and steam 2 to 3 minutes or until asparagus is tender and chicken is hot.

1 SERVING

Calories 460 (Calories from Fat 100); Total Fat 11g (Saturated Fat 2g); Cholesterol 70mg; Sodium 1,890mg; Total Carbohydrates 55g (Dietary Fiber 2g); Sugars 9g; Protein 35g

% Daily Value: Vitamin A 10%; Vitamin C 14%; Calcium 6%; Iron 22%

Exchanges: 3 Starch, 1 Vegetable, 3 1/2 Very Lean Meat, 2 Fat

Carbohydrate Choices: 3 1/2

QUICK FIX

Out of oyster sauce? Use 3/4 cup of the stir-fry sauce instead. Both oyster sauce and stir-fry sauce are found in the Asian foods section of the supermarket.

Chicken, Mushroom
and Asparagus Stir-Fry

Skillet Sweet-and-Sour Chicken

▪ ▪ ▪ ▪ Ready in 20 minutes

3 servings

1 package (12 oz.) frozen breaded cooked chicken nuggets
1 1/2 cups uncooked instant white rice
1 1/2 cups water
1 bag (1 lb. 5 oz.) frozen stir-fry vegetables with tangy
      sweet-and-sour sauce meal starter
1/4 cup cashews or peanuts, if desired

1. Cook chicken nuggets as directed on package.
2. Cook rice in water as directed on package.
3. Meanwhile, in 10-inch skillet, combine frozen vegetables, contents of pineapple pouch and frozen sauce from packet; mix well. Cover; cook over medium-high heat for 7 to 10 minutes or until vegetables are crisp-tender, stirring frequently.
4. Add cooked chicken; stir until well coated. Serve over cooked rice; sprinkle with cashews.

1 SERVING

Calories 680 (Calories from Fat 170); **Total Fat 19g (Saturated Fat 4g); Cholesterol 20mg; Sodium 1,350mg; Total Carbohydrates 108g (Dietary Fiber 7g); Sugars 29g; Protein 19g**

% Daily Value: **Vitamin A 70%; Vitamin C 20%; Calcium 10%; Iron 25%**

Exchanges: **3 1/2 Starch, 1/2 High-Fat Meat, 2 1/2 Fat, 3 Other Carbohydrates**

Carbohydrate Choices: **7**

QUICK FIX   Line the baking pan for the chicken nuggets with foil to save on cleanup.

Chili Turkey Tenderloins

■ ■ ■ **Ready in 25 minutes**

4 servings

1 lb. fresh turkey breast tenderloins, cut crosswise into
    1/2-inch slices
1/2 teaspoon salt
1/2 teaspoon cumin
1 cup frozen whole kernel corn (from 1-lb. bag)
1 cup chunky-style salsa
1/4 cup raisins
1/4 cup chili sauce
1/4 cup water

1. Sprinkle turkey slices with salt and cumin.
2. Heat 10-inch nonstick skillet over medium-high heat until hot. Add turkey; cook 2 to 4 minutes or until brown on both sides.
3. Add corn, salsa, raisins, chili sauce and water; mix well. Reduce heat to low; cover and simmer 8 to 10 minutes or until turkey is no longer pink in center and corn is hot, stirring occasionally.

1 SERVING

Calories 220 (Calories from Fat 10); Total Fat 1g (Saturated Fat 0g); Cholesterol 75mg; Sodium 1,010mg; Total Carbohydrates 23g (Dietary Fiber 2g); Sugars 13g; Protein 30g

% Daily Value: Vitamin A 10%; Vitamin C 6%; Calcium 4%; Iron 15%

Exchanges: 1/2 Starch, 1/2 Fruit, 4 Very Lean Meat, 1/2 Other Carbohydrate

Carbohydrate Choices: 1 1/2

QUICK FIX

For quick prep, look for disposable cutting sheets, available in packages of about 20, near the paper products at the discount or grocery store. These sheets are perfect for messy jobs like cutting meat. Just toss the used sheet when you're done!

Taco Turkey Medallions

■ ■ ■ ■ **Ready in 25 minutes**   *4 servings*

1 package (1.25 oz.) taco seasoning mix
2 tablespoons all-purpose flour
1 lb. fresh turkey breast tenderloins, cut crosswise
    into 1/2-inch slices
1 tablespoon olive or vegetable oil
1 cup chunky-style salsa
2 tablespoons honey
2 tablespoons chopped fresh cilantro, if desired

1 In large resealable food storage plastic bag, combine taco
    seasoning mix and flour; mix well. Add turkey slices; seal bag
    and shake to coat.

2 Heat oil in 10-inch nonstick skillet over medium-high heat
    until hot. Add turkey; cook until brown on both sides.

3 Add salsa, honey and any remaining coating mixture; mix
    well. Reduce heat to medium-low; cover and simmer 5 to 10
    minutes or until turkey is no longer pink in center, stirring
    occasionally. Sprinkle with cilantro.

1 SERVING

Calories 250 (Calories from Fat 45);
Total Fat 5g (Saturated Fat 1g);
Cholesterol 75mg; Sodium 1,320mg;
Total Carbohydrates 21g (Dietary
Fiber 1g); Sugars 11g; Protein 29g

% Daily Value: Vitamin A 8%;
Vitamin C 0%; Calcium 4%; Iron 15%

Exchanges: 1/2 Starch, 4 Very Lean Meat,
1 Other Carbohydrate
Carbohydrate Choices: 1 1/2

QUICK FIX

While the turkey simmers, cook some instant white rice to serve with the medallions.
It's the perfect side to soak up the delicious sauce!

Taco Turkey Medallions

Stir-Fried Lemon-Garlic Shrimp
White or Brown Rice
Broccoli, Carrots and Cauliflower
Apple and Grape Salad

4 servings

1. Cook instant white or brown rice.
2. While the rice cooks, make the salad.
3. Cook a bag of frozen broccoli, carrots and cauliflower in the microwave.
4. Make the stir-fried shrimp.

Apple and Grape Salad

1/2 teaspoon lemon juice
1/3 cup mayonnaise or salad dressing
1 medium apple, cubed (1 cup)
1/2 cup halved grapes
1/4 cup chopped celery
2 tablespoons chopped walnuts

1. In medium bowl, blend lemon juice and mayonnaise. Add remaining ingredients; stir gently to coat.
2. Serve immediately, or cover and refrigerate until serving time.

1 SERVING
Calories 190 (Calories from Fat 160);
Total Fat 17g (Saturated Fat 2g);
Cholesterol 10mg; Sodium 110mg;
Total Carbohydrates 9g (Dietary Fiber 1g);
Sugars 8g; Protein 1g
% Daily Value: Vitamin A 0%;
Vitamin C 8%; Calcium 0%; Iron 0%
Exchanges: 1/2 Fruit, 3 1/2 Fat
Carbohydrate Choices: 1/2

QUICK FIX

Use any nuts you may have on hand, such as pecans, almonds or peanuts. This salad is also tasty made with a cubed fresh pear instead of the apple.

Stir-Fried Lemon-Garlic Shrimp

1 tablespoon olive or vegetable oil
2 garlic cloves, minced, or 1/4 teaspoon
    garlic powder
1 lb. uncooked peeled deveined medium
    shrimp, tails removed
1/3 cup stir-fry sauce
4 medium green onions, sliced
    (1/4 cup)
2 teaspoons honey
1 teaspoon grated lemon peel
1 tablespoon lemon juice

1 In 10-inch nonstick skillet, heat oil over high heat until hot. Add garlic and shrimp; cook and stir 2 to 3 minutes or until shrimp are pink and firm.

2 Add all remaining ingredients; toss to mix. Cook 1 to 2 minutes or until sauce is of desired consistency.

QUICK FIX

Save prep time by purchasing the shrimp from the fish counter already shelled and deveined. Frozen shrimp can also be used in this recipe. Before cooking, thaw the shrimp and rinse with cold water to eliminate the salt used in processing.

1 SERVING

Calories 140 (Calories from Fat 35);
Total Fat 4g (Saturated Fat 1g);
Cholesterol 160mg; Sodium 890mg;
Total Carbohydrates 8g (Dietary Fiber 0g);
Sugars 4g; Protein 19g

% Daily Value: Vitamin A 4%;
Vitamin C 6%; Calcium 4%; Iron 15%

Exchanges: 2 1/2 Very Lean Meat, 1/2 Fat,
1/2 Other Carbohydrate

Carbohydrate Choices: 1/2

Fish with Carrots and Brown Rice

■ ■ ■ ■ ■ **Ready in 20 minutes**

4 servings

1 can (14 oz.) chicken broth
1 cup baby-cut carrots, quartered lengthwise
1 medium stalk celery, chopped (1/2 cup)
3 teaspoons dried parsley flakes
1 3/4 cups uncooked instant brown rice
1 lb. orange roughy fillets, sole, flounder or walleye pike
1/4 teaspoon garlic-pepper blend

1 In 12-inch nonstick skillet, combine broth, carrots, celery and parsley flakes. Bring to a boil. Reduce heat to medium-low; cover and cook 3 minutes.

2 Uncover skillet; return to a boil. Stir in rice. Top with orange roughy fillets; sprinkle with garlic-pepper blend. Reduce heat to medium-low; cover and cook 10 to 15 minutes or until liquid is absorbed and fish flakes easily with fork.

1 SERVING

Calories 440 (Calories from Fat 45); Total Fat 5g (Saturated Fat 1g); Cholesterol 60mg; Sodium 580mg; Total Carbohydrates 67g (Dietary Fiber 6g); Sugars 2g; Protein 32g

% Daily Value: Vitamin A 100%; Vitamin C 2%; Calcium 6%; Iron 12%

Exchanges: 4 Starch, 3 Very Lean Meat, 1/2 Fat

Carbohydrate Choices: 4

QUICK FIX

Store fresh fish, such as orange roughy, tightly wrapped in the coldest part of the refrigerator for no longer than 2 days.

Dilly Tuna Patties

■ ■ ■ ■ **Ready in 25 minutes**

4 servings

Patties

1 egg
2 tablespoons Dijon mustard
3/4 cup unseasoned dry bread crumbs
1/4 cup finely chopped onion
1/4 cup dill pickle relish
2 tablespoons drained chopped pimientos
1 can (12 oz.) tuna in water, drained, flaked

Sauce

1/2 cup mayonnaise or salad dressing
2 teaspoons dill pickle relish
1/4 teaspoon lemon-pepper seasoning

1 In medium bowl, beat egg. Add all remaining patty ingredients; mix well. Shape mixture into 4 (3/4-inch-thick) patties.

2 Heat 12-inch nonstick skillet over medium-high heat until hot. Add patties; cook 6 to 8 minutes or until golden brown on both sides.

3 In small bowl, combine all sauce ingredients; mix well. Serve tuna patties with sauce and, if desired, additional pickle relish.

1 SERVING
Calories 400 (Calories from Fat 230);
Total Fat 25g (Saturated Fat 4g);
Cholesterol 90mg; Sodium 970mg;
Total Carbohydrates 21g (Dietary
Fiber 1g); Sugars 2g; Protein 23g
% Daily Value: Vitamin A 8%;
Vitamin C 10%; Calcium 6%; Iron 15%
Exchanges: 1 1/2 Starch, 2 1/2 Very Lean
Meat, 4 1/2 Fat
Carbohydrate Choices: 1 1/2

QUICK FIX

Pressed for time? Just substitute prepared tartar sauce for the sauce in the recipe. Look for it in jars near the other condiments at the grocery store.

Jump Start with Pasta

Superfast Ready in 15 minutes or less

Skillet Beefy Chili Mac

Ready in 25 minutes

4 servings (1 1/2 cups each)

1 1/2 cups uncooked elbow macaroni (6 oz.)
1 lb. lean (at least 80%) ground beef
1 can (15 oz.) spicy chili beans, undrained
1 can (14.5 oz.) diced zesty chili-style tomatoes, undrained
1/4 teaspoon salt
1/4 teaspoon pepper
1 cup shredded Cheddar cheese (4 oz.)

1. Cook macaroni as directed on package. Drain; return to saucepan. Cover to keep warm.
2. Meanwhile, in 12-inch nonstick skillet, cook ground beef over medium-high heat for 5 to 7 minutes or until brown, stirring frequently. Drain.
3. Reduce heat to medium. Stir in cooked macaroni, beans, tomatoes, salt and pepper. Cook an additional 3 to 5 minutes or until bubbly, stirring frequently. Sprinkle with cheese.

1 SERVING

Calories 595 (Calories from Fat 245); Total Fat 27g (Saturated Fat 13g); Cholesterol 95mg; Sodium 1,490mg; Total Carbohydrates 55g (Dietary Fiber 7g); Sugars 6g; Protein 40g

% Daily Value: Vitamin A 22%; Vitamin C 20%; Calcium 22%; Iron 34%

Exchanges: 3 Starch, 4 1/2 Medium-Fat Meat, 1 Fat

Carbohydrate Choices: 0

QUICK FIX

If you don't have a can of zesty chili-style tomatoes on hand, use a can of plain diced tomatoes and add 1/2 teaspoon chili powder.

Fettuccine with Beef and Peppers
Italian Mixed Salad
Strawberry-Bananas with Chocolate Sauce   *4 servings*

1. Make the salad except for the oil and vinegar.
2. Make the fettuccine with beef and peppers.
3. Drizzle the salad with the oil and vinegar.
4. For dessert, drizzle chocolate sauce over fresh strawberries and sliced bananas.

Italian Mixed Salad

4 cups bite-size pieces romaine lettuce
1 jar (6 oz.) marinated quartered artichoke hearts, drained
1 jar (6 oz.) whole mushrooms, drained
2 Italian plum tomatoes, cut into small wedges
1/2 small cucumber, halved lengthwise, seeded and sliced
1/4 cup olive oil
2 tablespoons red wine vinegar

1. In large bowl, combine all ingredients except oil and vinegar; toss to mix.
2. Drizzle salad with oil and vinegar; toss gently to coat.

1 SERVING
Calories 180 (Calories from Fat 140);
Total Fat 15g (Saturated Fat 2g);
Cholesterol 0mg; Sodium 320mg; Total
Carbohydrates 10g (Dietary Fiber 5g);
Sugars 4g; Protein 4g
% Daily Value: Vitamin A 30%;
Vitamin C 40%; Calcium 4%; Iron 10%
Exchanges: 2 Vegetable, 3 Fat
Carbohydrate Choices: 0

QUICK FIX
Use 1/4 cup of your favorite Italian salad dressing instead of the olive oil and red wine vinegar for a slightly different flavor.

Fettuccine with Beef and Peppers

1 package (9 oz.) refrigerated fettuccine
1 lb. lean (at least 80%) ground beef
1 medium green bell pepper, cut into thin bite-size
    strips
1 medium red bell pepper, cut into thin bite-size
    strips
1/2 cup half-and-half
1/3 cup basil pesto
1/2 teaspoon salt
1/8 teaspoon pepper

1. Cook fettuccine as directed on package.
   Drain; cover to keep warm.

2. Meanwhile, in 10-inch skillet, cook ground beef
   over medium-high heat for 5 to 7 minutes or until
   thoroughly cooked, stirring frequently. Drain. Add bell
   peppers; cook 4 to 6 minutes or until crisp-tender, stirring
   occasionally.

3. Add half-and-half, pesto, salt, pepper and cooked fettuccine.
   Reduce heat to medium; cook an additional 3 to 5 minutes or until
   thoroughly heated, stirring occasionally.

QUICK FIX

On days when you are pressed for time, use a package of frozen
mixed bell pepper and onion stir-fry as a substitute for the bell
peppers in this recipe. The onions in the mix will add just a bit of
additional flavor!

1 SERVING
Calories 560 (Calories from Fat 280);
Total Fat 31g (Saturated Fat 10g);
Cholesterol 150mg; Sodium 510mg;
Total Carbohydrates 40g (Dietary
Fiber 2g); Sugars 5g; Protein 31g
% Daily Value: Vitamin A 30%;
Vitamin C 60%; Calcium 10%; Iron 25%
Exchanges: 2 1/2 Starch, 3 1/2 Medium-Fat
Meat, 2 1/2 Fat
Carbohydrate Choices: 0

Beef and Ramen Noodle Bowls

■ ■ ■ Ready in 20 minutes

4 servings (1 1/2 cups each)

1 tablespoon vegetable oil
1 medium onion, cut into thin wedges
1 bag (1 lb. 5 oz.) frozen stir-fry vegetables with
    traditional teriyaki sauce meal starter
3/4 cup water
1 tablespoon peanut butter
1 package (3 oz.) oriental-flavor ramen noodle soup mix
3/4 lb. cooked roast beef (from deli), cut into thin
    bite-size strips
1/4 cup chopped peanuts

1. In 10-inch skillet, heat oil over medium-high heat until hot. Add onion; cook and stir 1 minute. Add frozen sauce from meal starter, water, peanut butter and 1 teaspoon of the seasoning from soup mix; discard remaining seasoning. Cook 2 to 3 minutes or until sauce is thawed, stirring occasionally.

2. Break up ramen noodles (from soup mix) into skillet. Add frozen vegetables; cover and cook an additional 8 to 10 minutes or until vegetables are crisp-tender, stirring occasionally.

3. Add beef; cook and stir until thoroughly heated. Spoon mixture into individual serving bowls. Sprinkle with peanuts.

1 SERVING

Calories 340 (Calories from Fat 145); Total Fat 16g (Saturated Fat 3g); Cholesterol 40mg; Sodium 1,850mg; Total Carbohydrates 30g (Dietary Fiber 5g); Sugars 11g; Protein 24g

% Daily Value: Vitamin A 14%; Vitamin C 26%; Calcium 4%; Iron 16%

Exchanges: 1 Starch, 1 Vegetable, 3 Lean Meat, 1 1/2 Fat

Carbohydrate Choices: 0

QUICK FIX

To easily break up the ramen noodles before adding them to the skillet, gently pound the unopened package with a rolling pin or wooden spoon.

Beef and Ramen Noodle Bowls

Skillet Meatballs with Linguine
Corn with Chives
Mixed Greens with Raspberry Vinaigrette
Cookies and Ice Cream

4 servings

1 Cook the linguine and meatballs.

2 While the linguine and meatballs cook, make the corn.

3 Toss a purchased bag of mixed salad greens with raspberry vinaigrette. Sprinkle with sliced almonds.

4 For dessert, serve purchased cookies with bowls of ice cream.

Corn with Chives

1 package (1 lb.) frozen corn
2 tablespoons chopped fresh chives or 2 teaspoons
 freeze-dried chopped chives
2 tablespoons butter or margarine
3 tablespoons half-and-half or milk
1/4 teaspoon salt
Dash pepper

1 Cook corn as directed on package. Drain; return to saucepan.

2 Stir in remaining ingredients. Cook 1 to 2 minutes or until thoroughly heated.

1 SERVING
Calories **160 (Calories from Fat 70);
Total Fat 7g (Saturated Fat 2g);
Cholesterol 5mg; Sodium 220mg;
Total Carbohydrates 22g (Dietary
Fiber 3g); Sugars 3g; Protein 3g**
% Daily Value: **Vitamin A 10%;
Vitamin C 4%; Calcium 0%; Iron 2%**
Exchanges: **1 1/2 Starch, 1 Fat**
Carbohydrate Choices: **0**

QUICK FIX

Use a 14-ounce can of cream-style corn instead of the frozen corn to save a few minutes of cook time. Just add the chives to the cream-style corn and heat on the stovetop or in the microwave.

Skillet Meatballs with Linguine

8 oz. uncooked linguine

1 package (10.5 oz.) frozen cooked light Italian meatballs

1 can (15 oz.) Italian-style tomato sauce

1 can (10.75 oz.) condensed 98% fat-free cream of mushroom soup with 30% less sodium

1 jar (2.5 oz.) sliced mushrooms, drained

1/4 cup chopped fresh parsley, if desired

1. Cook linguine as directed on package. Drain; cover to keep warm.

2. Meanwhile, in 10-inch skillet, combine all remaining ingredients except parsley; mix well. Bring to a boil over medium-high heat. Reduce heat to medium-low; cover and cook 8 to 10 minutes or until meatballs are thoroughly heated, stirring occasionally.

3. Serve meatballs with sauce over cooked linguine. Sprinkle with parsley.

1 SERVING
Calories 430 (Calories from Fat 90);
Total Fat 10g (Saturated Fat 4g);
Cholesterol 30mg; Sodium 1,250mg;
Total Carbohydrates 61g (Dietary Fiber 5g);
Sugars 12g; Protein 25g
% Daily Value: Vitamin A 10%;
Vitamin C 10%; Calcium 20%; Iron 25%
Exchanges: 3 Starch, 1/2 Fruit, 1 Vegetable,
2 Medium-Fat Meat
Carbohydrate Choices: 0

QUICK FIX

You can use one 9-ounce package of refrigerated linguine instead of the dried type because it cooks much quicker. Just follow the package directions—it cooks in just a couple of minutes

Beef and Pasta Alfredo

■ ■ ■ ■ **Ready in 25 minutes**

5 servings (1 1/2 cups each)

2 1/4 cups uncooked penne pasta (8 oz.)
1 lb. lean (at least 80%) ground beef
3 medium green onions, sliced (3 tablespoons)
1 container (10 oz.) refrigerated Alfredo pasta sauce
4 medium Italian plum tomatoes, quartered, sliced (1 1/2 cups)
2 tablespoons chopped fresh or 1 1/2 teaspoons dried basil

1 Cook penne as directed on package. Drain; cover to keep warm.

2 Meanwhile, in 10-inch skillet, cook ground beef over medium-high heat for 5 to 7 minutes or until thoroughly cooked, stirring frequently. Drain.

3 Stir in onions and Alfredo sauce. Reduce heat to medium; cook 3 to 5 minutes or until bubbly, stirring occasionally.

4 Add cooked penne, tomatoes and basil; cook an additional 3 to 5 minutes or until thoroughly heated, stirring occasionally. If desired, add salt and freshly ground pepper to taste.

1 SERVING

Calories 540 (Calories from Fat 280); Total Fat 31g (Saturated Fat 15g); Cholesterol 95mg; Sodium 300mg; Total Carbohydrates 40g (Dietary Fiber 2g); Sugars 4g; Protein 25g

% Daily Value: Vitamin A 4%; Vitamin C 8%; Calcium 10%; Iron 20%

Exchanges: 2 1/2 Starch, 2 1/2 Medium-Fat Meat, 3 1/2 Fat

Carbohydrate Choices: 0

QUICK FIX

Use the same pan to cook the whole dish. Just cook and drain the pasta and let it stand in the colander while you cook the remaining ingredients in the same Dutch oven. Add the pasta and tomatoes to the ground beef mixture, and continue heating.

Easy Ham and Noodles

■ ■ ■ ■ Ready in 20 minutes

4 servings (1 3/4 cups each)

1 can (14 oz.) chicken broth
1 cup water
3 cups uncooked dumpling egg noodles (6 oz.)
2 packages (10 oz.) frozen broccoli, cauliflower
    and carrots in cheese-flavored sauce
2 cups cubed cooked ham

1. In medium saucepan, bring broth and water to a boil. Add noodles; return to a boil. Cook 8 to 10 minutes or until noodles are tender and most of liquid is absorbed. Do not drain.
2. Meanwhile, cook vegetables as directed on package.
3. Add vegetables in cheese sauce and ham to noodle mixture; toss gently to mix.

1 SERVING

Calories 350 (Calories from Fat 100);
Total Fat 11g (Saturated Fat 4g);
Cholesterol 80mg; Sodium 2,090mg;
Total Carbohydrates 38g (Dietary
Fiber 3g); Sugars 4g; Protein 25g

% Daily Value: Vitamin A 26%;
Vitamin C 22%; Calcium 6%; Iron 16%

Exchanges: 2 Starch, 2 Vegetable, 2 Lean
Meat, 1 Fat

Carbohydrate Choices: 0

QUICK FIX

For a change, use 2 cups cubed cooked chicken or turkey for the ham. Pick up a rotisserie chicken or cooked turkey or chicken from the deli. You'll need about a pound of deli meat

Caesar Tortellini with Ham

■ ■ ■ **Ready in 20 minutes**

4 servings

1 package (9 oz.) refrigerated cheese-filled tortellini
1 1/2 cups frozen broccoli florets (from 14-oz. bag)
1 1/2 cups cubed cooked ham
2/3 cup creamy Caesar salad dressing
3 cups shredded romaine lettuce (from 10-oz. bag)
2 tablespoons shredded Parmesan cheese

1. In 3-quart saucepan, bring 2 quarts (8 cups) water to a boil. Add tortellini and broccoli; cook as directed on tortellini package until tortellini are tender. Drain; return to saucepan.

2. Add ham and salad dressing; stir gently to mix. Cook over medium-low heat just until thoroughly heated, stirring occasionally.

3. Arrange lettuce on individual plates. Spoon tortellini mixture over lettuce. Sprinkle with cheese.

1 SERVING

Calories 375 (Calories from Fat 225);
Total Fat 25g (Saturated Fat 7g);
Cholesterol 100mg; Sodium 1,250mg;
Total Carbohydrates 17g (Dietary
Fiber 3g); Sugars 3g; Protein 21g

% Daily Value: Vitamin A 46%;
Vitamin C 30%; Calcium 18%; Iron 14%

Exchanges: 1 Starch, 1 Vegetable,
2 1/2 Lean Meat, 3 1/2 Fat

Carbohydrate Choices: 0

QUICK FIX

To minimize preparation time, purchase cubed cooked ham. It's available in packages near the other refrigerated cooked meats.

Ice is nice, but don't limit yourself to plain old water when it comes to filling your ice-cube trays. Try these simple ideas instead. (After you freeze the cubes, pop them in a plastic food-storage bag and seal.)

<u>1.</u> Freeze leftover chicken broth, beef broth or wine to use later in casseroles, soups and sauces.

<u>2.</u> More pesto than people? Freeze leftovers in cubes to toss into soups, stews and casseroles for quick added flavor.

<u>3.</u> Freeze small fresh berries in ice cubes to add a festive and flavorful touch to fruity drinks.

<u>4.</u> Here's a good way to use up any extra lemons or limes: Put lemon or lime halves or wedges in a resealable plastic food-storage bag and seal. Use your hand to squeeze the juice out. Snip off a corner of the bag, squeeze the juice into an ice-cube tray and freeze. (One cube is equal to about 1 tablespoon of juice.)

<u>5.</u> Put leftover chopped herbs, such as parsley, sage, rosemary or thyme, into an ice-cube tray. Fill the tray with water and freeze. (A good ratio to shoot for is 2 tablespoons herbs to about 1 tablespoon water.) Add to soups, stews and sauces.

Ice-Cube Tray

Basil-Pork and Asian Noodles

■ ■ ■ ■ **Ready in 25 minutes**

4 servings

8 oz. uncooked capellini (angel hair) pasta
2 teaspoons sesame oil
1 tablespoon sesame seed
1 lb. pork tenderloin, halved lengthwise, thinly sliced
1 medium onion, cut into thin wedges
1/2 cup stir-fry sauce
2 tablespoons honey
2 cups frozen sugar snap peas (from 1-lb. bag)
1/4 cup sliced fresh basil

1. Cook pasta as directed on package. Drain; return to saucepan. Add sesame oil; toss to coat. Cover to keep warm.

2. Meanwhile, heat 10-inch nonstick skillet over medium-high heat until hot. Add sesame seed; cook and stir 2 to 3 minutes or until golden brown. (Watch carefully to prevent burning.) Remove from skillet.

3. In same skillet, cook pork and onion over medium-high heat for 3 to 4 minutes or until no longer pink, stirring frequently.

4. Add stir-fry sauce, honey and sugar snap peas; mix well. Reduce heat to medium; cook 3 to 4 minutes or until peas are crisp-tender, stirring occasionally. Add basil; cook and stir 1 minute. Serve pork mixture over cooked pasta. Sprinkle with toasted sesame seed.

1 SERVING

Calories 500 (Calories from Fat 80); Total Fat 9g (Saturated Fat 2g); Cholesterol 70mg; Sodium 1,660mg; Total Carbohydrates 67g (Dietary Fiber 5g); Sugars 18g; Protein 38g

% Daily Value: Vitamin A 8%; Vitamin C 28%; Calcium 6%; Iron 32%

Exchanges: 4 Starch, 1 Vegetable, 3 1/2 Lean Meat

Carbohydrate Choices: 0

QUICK FIX

Speed up this meal even more by using refrigerated angel hair pasta. A 9-ounce package is just right, and it cooks in less than half the time of dried pasta.

Basil-Pork and Asian Noodles

Tuna and Ham with Fettuccine

■ ■ ■ ■ Ready in 20 minutes   *4 servings*

8 oz. uncooked fettuccine
1 cup frozen small sweet peas (from 1-lb. bag)
4 oz. cream cheese, softened
1/2 cup milk
1/2 teaspoon salt
1/8 teaspoon pepper
1/2 cup cooked ham strips (2 × 1/4 × 1/4-inch)
1 can (6 oz.) white tuna in water, drained, flaked

1 Cook fettuccine as directed on package, adding peas during last 4 minutes of cooking time. Drain; rinse with cold water. Drain well; set aside.

2 In same saucepan, heat cream cheese over low heat until melted. Gradually add milk, stirring until blended. Stir in salt and pepper. Add cooked fettuccine; mix well. Add ham and tuna; stir gently to mix.

3 Cook over medium heat until thoroughly heated, stirring occasionally.

1 SERVING

Calories 400 (Calories from Fat 130); Total Fat 15g (Saturated Fat 8g); Cholesterol 105mg; Sodium 1,060mg; Total Carbohydrates 44g (Dietary Fiber 3g); Sugars 4g; Protein 26g

% Daily Value: Vitamin A 15%; Vitamin C 2%; Calcium 10%; Iron 25%

Exchanges: 3 Starch, 2 1/2 Lean Meat, 1 Fat

Carbohydrate Choices: 0

QUICK FIX

Get ahold of your pasta with a handy pasta fork available at kitchen specialty stores. This handy gadget is not only great for serving pasta, but if you find one with a hole in the center, you can also perfectly measure 8 ounces of long pasta such as fettuccine or spaghetti.

Ravioli with Broccoli, Tomatoes and Mushrooms

■ ■ ■ **Ready in 20 minutes**

4 servings (1 1/2 cups each)

1 package (25 oz.) frozen Italian sausage-filled ravioli
1 cup frozen cut broccoli (from 1-lb. bag)
1 can (14.5 oz.) diced tomatoes with basil, garlic and oregano, undrained
1 jar (4.5 oz.) sliced mushrooms, drained
1/4 cup shredded Parmesan cheese (1 oz.)

1. In 3-quart saucepan, bring 2 quarts (8 cups) water to a boil. Add ravioli and broccoli; cook 5 minutes or until ravioli are floating and broccoli is crisp-tender. Drain well in colander; set aside.

2. Add tomatoes to same saucepan. Bring to a boil. Cook over medium heat for 3 to 5 minutes or until slightly thickened, stirring occasionally. Add cooked ravioli, broccoli and mushrooms; cook until thoroughly heated, stirring frequently. Sprinkle with cheese.

1 SERVING

Calories 440 (Calories from Fat 80);
Total Fat 9g (Saturated Fat 3g);
Cholesterol 20mg; **Sodium** 830mg;
Total Carbohydrates 69g (Dietary Fiber 5g); **Sugars** 6g; **Protein** 20g

% Daily Value: **Vitamin A** 15%;
Vitamin C 25%; **Calcium** 70%; **Iron** 8%

Exchanges: 4 Starch, 1 Vegetable, 1 High-Fat Meat

Carbohydrate Choices: 0

QUICK FIX

Water boils faster if the lid is on and if the water is unsalted, so add the salt after it comes to a boil.

Penne with Cheesy Tomato-Sausage Sauce

4 servings

2 2/3 cups uncooked penne pasta (8 oz.)
1/2 lb. bulk Italian pork sausage
1 container (15 oz.) refrigerated tomato pasta sauce
1/4 cup thinly sliced fresh basil
2 oz. mozzarella cheese, diced (1/2 cup)
1/4 cup shredded Parmesan cheese (1 oz.)

1. Cook penne as directed on package. Drain; cover to keep warm.
2. Meanwhile, in 3-quart saucepan, cook sausage until no longer pink, stirring frequently. Drain; return to saucepan. Add pasta sauce; bring to a boil. Reduce heat to medium-low. Stir in basil and mozzarella cheese. Cook 1 to 2 minutes or until cheese is slightly melted, stirring occasionally.
3. Serve sauce mixture over cooked penne. Sprinkle with Parmesan cheese.

1 SERVING

Calories 500 (Calories from Fat 170); Total Fat 19g (Saturated Fat 6g); Cholesterol 45mg; Sodium 1,010mg; Total Carbohydrates 59g (Dietary Fiber 4g); Sugars 12g; Protein 23g

% Daily Value: Vitamin A 20%; Vitamin C 6%; Calcium 25%; Iron 25%

Exchanges: 3 Starch, 2 High-Fat Meat

Carbohydrate Choices: 0

QUICK FIX

In a hurry and don't have the fresh basil? Just substitute about 1 teaspoon dried basil leaves instead.

Penne with Cheesy Tomato-Sausage

Chicken Puttanesca Sauté

4 servings

8 oz. uncooked capellini (angel hair) pasta
1 lb. chicken breast tenders
1/4 teaspoon salt
1/8 teaspoon pepper
1 tablespoon olive oil
1 can (14.5 oz.) diced tomatoes with roasted garlic, undrained
1/2 cup sliced green olives
1/8 teaspoon crushed red pepper flakes
1 can (14.5 oz.) cut wax or green beans, drained

1 Cook pasta as directed on package. Drain well; cover to keep warm.

2 Meanwhile, pat chicken tenders dry with paper towels; sprinkle with salt and pepper. In 10-inch nonstick skillet, heat oil over medium-high heat until hot. Add chicken; cook 4 to 6 minutes or until lightly brown on both sides.

3 Add tomatoes, olives and pepper flakes; cook 4 to 6 minutes or until chicken is no longer pink in center and liquid has been reduced slightly. Add beans; cook an additional 2 to 3 minutes or until beans are thoroughly heated.

4 Serve chicken mixture over cooked angel hair pasta.

1 SERVING

Calories 450 (Calories from Fat 90);
Total Fat 10g (Saturated Fat 2g);
Cholesterol 70mg; Sodium 1,250mg;
Total Carbohydrates 55g (Dietary
Fiber 4g); Sugars 6g; Protein 35g

% Daily Value: Vitamin A 10%;
Vitamin C 16%; Calcium 8%; Iron 26%

Exchanges: 3 Starch, 2 Vegetable, 3 Very
Lean Meat, 1 1/2 Fat

Carbohydrate Choices: 0

QUICK FIX

If you don't have a can of diced tomatoes with roasted garlic, use a can of diced tomatoes and add 1/4 teaspoon garlic powder.

Chicken Puttanesca Sauté

Two-Cheese Chicken with Couscous

■ ■ ■ ■ **Ready in 25 minutes**

6 servings

Chicken Mixture
1 tablespoon vegetable or olive oil
1 1/4 lb. boneless skinless chicken breast halves,
    cut into 1/2- to 3/4-inch pieces
1/2 teaspoon garlic-pepper blend
1 jar (26 to 28 oz.) chunky pasta sauce
1 jar (4.5 oz.) sliced mushrooms, drained
3/4 cup shredded mozzarella cheese (3 oz.)

Couscous
2 cups water
1 cup uncooked couscous
1/2 teaspoon garlic-pepper blend
1/4 teaspoon salt
1/4 cup grated Parmesan cheese

1. In 10-inch skillet, heat oil over medium-high heat until hot. Add chicken; sprinkle with 1/2 teaspoon garlic-pepper blend. Cook 2 to 4 minutes or until brown, stirring frequently.
2. Add pasta sauce and mushrooms. Bring to a boil. Reduce heat to medium; cook 5 to 7 minutes or until sauce is of desired consistency and chicken is no longer pink in center, stirring occasionally.
3. Meanwhile, bring water to a boil. Remove from heat. Stir in couscous, 1/2 teaspoon garlic-pepper blend and salt; mix well. Cover; let stand 5 minutes.
4. Stir mozzarella cheese into chicken mixture. Fluff couscous with fork; stir in Parmesan cheese. Serve chicken mixture over couscous. If desired, sprinkle with additional Parmesan cheese.

1 SERVING
Calories 410 (Calories from Fat 110);
Total Fat 12g (Saturated Fat 3g);
Cholesterol 65mg; Sodium 970mg;
Total Carbohydrates 44g (Dietary
Fiber 5g); Sugars 13g; Protein 32g
% Daily Value: Vitamin A 25%;
Vitamin C 4%; Calcium 25%; Iron 15%
Exchanges: 2 1/2 Starch, 3 1/2 Lean Meat
Carbohydrate Choices: 0

QUICK FIX

Chicken tenders will shorten preparation time for this recipe. Cut them into 1/2 - to 3/4-inch pieces. Look for the tenders near other cut and packaged chicken in the meat department.

Southwest Chicken and Fettuccine

■ ■ ■ ■ **Ready in 20 minutes**

4 servings (1 1/2 cups each)

1 package (9 oz.) refrigerated fettuccine
1 can (14.5 oz.) diced tomatoes with green chiles
   or jalapeño chiles, undrained
1 package (9 oz.) frozen southwestern-flavored cooked
   chicken breast strips, thawed
1 cup shredded Monterey Jack cheese (4 oz.)
1 medium avocado, pitted, peeled and chopped, if desired

1 Cook fettuccine in 3-quart saucepan as directed on package. Drain in colander; cover to keep warm.

2 In same saucepan, combine tomatoes and chicken; mix well. Cook over medium heat until thoroughly heated, stirring occasionally. Stir in cooked fettuccine. Sprinkle individual servings with cheese and avocado.

1 SERVING

Calories 405 (Calories from Fat 170);
Total Fat 19g (Saturated Fat 8g);
Cholesterol 100mg; Sodium 830mg;
Total Carbohydrates 27g (Dietary Fiber 3g);
Sugars 6g; Protein 31g

% Daily Value: Vitamin A 12%;
Vitamin C 12%; Calcium 24%; Iron 14%

Exchanges: 1 1/2 Starch, 1 Vegetable,
3 1/2 Lean Meat, 1 1/2 Fat

Carbohydrate Choices: 2

QUICK FIX

Here's an easy way to chop an avocado. After cutting the avocado into halves and removing the pit, chop it right in the peel. Use the tip of the knife blade to score the avocado halves in a crisscross pattern, cutting just to the peel. Run a small spoon next to the peel, rotating the avocado and squeezing slightly to release the chopped fruit.

Tortellini with Chicken
Lettuce Wedge with French Dressing
Strawberry-Rhubarb Sundaes

6 servings

1 Make the strawberry-rhubarb sauce for the sundaes; let stand at room temperature.

2 While the sauce cooks, cut a head of iceberg lettuce into 6 wedges; serve with dressing.

3 Make the tortellini with chicken.

4 For dessert, make the sundaes.

Strawberry-Rhubarb Sundaes

2 cups sliced fresh or frozen rhubarb
1/2 cup sugar
1/4 cup water
1 package (10 oz.) frozen strawberries in syrup
6 individual sponge cake cups
1 1/2 pints (3 cups) vanilla frozen yogurt or ice cream

1 In medium saucepan, combine rhubarb, sugar and water; mix well. Bring to a boil. Reduce heat to medium-low; simmer 5 minutes, stirring occasionally.

2 Add strawberries; cook and stir 1 to 2 minutes or until berries are thawed.

3 To serve, place sponge cake cups on individual dessert plates or dish. Place 1/2 cup frozen yogurt in each cake cup. Spoon about 1/3 cup warm strawberry-rhubarb sauce over each.

1 SERVING
Calories 290 (Calories from Fat 20);
Total Fat 2g (Saturated Fat 1g);
Cholesterol 45mg; Sodium 70mg;
Total Carbohydrates 61g (Dietary
Fiber 2g); Sugars 52g; Protein 6g
% Daily Value: Vitamin A 4%;
Vitamin C 20%; Calcium 25%; Iron 4%
Exchanges: 1 Skim Milk, 3 1/2 Other
Carbohydrates
Carbohydrate Choices: 4

QUICK FIX

You can make the strawberry-rhubarb sauce ahead and keep it in the refrigerator. Just reheat in the microwave, or serve it cold.

Tortellini with Chicken

1 tablespoon butter or margarine
1/4 cup Italian-style dry bread crumbs
1 package (9 oz.) frozen diced cooked
   chicken breast
1 bag (19 oz.) frozen cheese-filled
   tortellini
1 box (9 oz.) frozen asparagus cuts in a
   pouch
1 jar (16 oz.) Alfredo pasta sauce
2 tablespoons shredded Parmesan
   cheese

1 In Dutch oven, bring 3 quarts (12 cups)
water to a boil. Meanwhile, in medium
microwavable bowl, combine butter and bread
crumbs. Microwave on High for
1 minute, stirring every 15 seconds until butter is melted. Heat
chicken in microwave according to package directions.

2 Add tortellini to boiling water; return to a boil. Reduce heat to
medium. Add asparagus from pouch; simmer 3 minutes or until
tortellini are tender. Drain and reserve.

3 In same Dutch oven, add chicken and Alfredo sauce. Cook over
medium heat 2 to 3 minutes until heated through. Gently mix in
tortellini and asparagus.

4 To serve, sprinkle with bread crumbs and Parmesan cheese.

1 SERVING

Calories 530 (Calories from Fat 315);
Total Fat 35g (Saturated Fat 20g);
Cholesterol 195mg; Sodium 640mg;
Total Carbohydrates 26g (Dietary Fiber
1g); Sugars 3g; Protein 28g

% Daily Value: Vitamin A 32%;
Vitamin C 8%; Calcium 30%; Iron 12%

Exchanges: 2 Starch, 3 Lean Meat, 5 Fat

Carbohydrate Choices: 2

QUICK FIX

Try 1/4 cup of finely crushed corn flake cereal or corn chips for the bread
crumbs. Just microwave with the butter

Creamy Chicken and Asparagus

■ ■ ■ ■ **Ready in 20 minutes**

4 servings (1 1/4 cups each)

1 box (9 oz.) frozen asparagus cuts in a pouch
1 package (1.8 oz.) leek soup, dip and recipe mix
2 1/2 cups water
2 cups uncooked small pasta shells (8 oz.)
1 package (9 oz.) frozen diced cooked chicken breast
1 cup sour cream
1/4 cup shredded Parmesan cheese (1 oz.)

1. Cook asparagus as directed on package.
2. Meanwhile, in 2-quart saucepan, combine soup mix and water. Bring to a boil. Reduce heat to low. Add pasta; simmer 8 to 10 minutes or until pasta is tender, stirring occasionally.
3. Add chicken, sour cream and cooked asparagus; stir gently to mix. Cook 3 to 5 minutes or until thoroughly heated, stirring occasionally. Sprinkle with cheese.

1 SERVING

Calories 520 (Calories from Fat 155);
Total Fat 17g (Saturated Fat 9g);
Cholesterol 100mg; Sodium 1,310mg;
Total Carbohydrates 58g
(Dietary Fiber 3g); Sugars 9g; Protein 34g

% Daily Value: Vitamin A 18%;
Vitamin C 16%; Calcium 20%; Iron 18%

Exchanges: 4 Starch, 3 Very Lean Meat, 3 Fat

Carbohydrate Choices: 4

QUICK FIX

No frozen chicken in your freezer? You can use 1 cup chopped leftover cooked chicken, turkey or ham that you might have on hand. Or pick up about 8 ounces from the deli.

Lemon-Chicken Primavera

6 servings (1 1/2 cups each)

1 package (12 oz.) uncooked fettuccine
1 tablespoon olive oil
2 garlic cloves, minced or 1/4 teaspoon garlic powder
1 package (9 oz.) frozen grilled cooked chicken breast strips
1 lb. fresh asparagus spears, trimmed, cut into 1 1/2-inch pieces
1 1/2 cups baby-cut carrots, quartered lengthwise
1 teaspoon lemon-pepper seasoning
2 cups chicken broth
2 tablespoons cornstarch
2 tablespoons chopped fresh or 1 1/2 teaspoons dried basil
2 teaspoons grated lemon peel
1/3 cup shredded Parmesan cheese (1 1/3 oz.)

1. In 3- to 4-quart saucepan, cook fettuccine as directed on package. Drain; return to saucepan. Cover to keep warm.

2. Meanwhile, in 10-inch skillet, heat oil over medium-high heat until hot. Add garlic; cook and stir 30 to 60 seconds or until softened. Add chicken, asparagus, carrots and lemon-pepper seasoning. Reserve 1/4 cup of the broth; stir remaining broth into chicken mixture. Bring to a boil. Reduce heat to medium; cover and cook 5 minutes or until vegetables are crisp-tender, stirring occasionally.

3. In small bowl, mix reserved 1/4 cup broth and cornstarch until smooth. Add to skillet; cook and stir until thickened. Stir in basil and lemon peel.

4. Pour chicken mixture over cooked fettuccine in saucepan; toss to coat. Sprinkle individual servings with cheese.

1 SERVING

Calories 450 (Calories from Fat 110); Total Fat 12g (Saturated Fat 3g); Cholesterol 105mg; Sodium 1,120mg; Total Carbohydrates 54g (Dietary Fiber 3g); Sugars 3g; Protein 31g

% Daily Value: Vitamin A 100%; Vitamin C 12%; Calcium 14%; Iron 22%

Exchanges: 3 1/2 Starch, 3 Very Lean Meat, 2 Fat

Carbohydrate Choices: 3 1/2

QUICK FIX

Look for jars of chopped garlic in the produce department. You'll need 1 teaspoon of the chopped garlic or use the amount as directed on the label for the equivalent of 2 cloves.

Ravioli with Corn and Cilantro

3 servings (1 1/4 cups each)

1 package (9 oz.) refrigerated roasted-chicken-and-garlic-filled
    or cheese-filled ravioli
2 tablespoons olive oil
2 garlic cloves, minced, or 1/4 teaspoon garlic powder
1 can (11 oz.) whole kernel corn with red and green
    peppers, drained
1/4 teaspoon salt
1/4 cup chopped fresh cilantro

1. Cook ravioli as directed on package. Drain.
2. Meanwhile, in large skillet, heat oil over medium heat until
   hot. Add garlic; cook and stir 2 to 3 minutes or until tender.
   Add corn and salt; cook until thoroughly heated, stirring
   occasionally.
3. Add cooked ravioli; toss to coat. Sprinkle with cilantro.

1 SERVING

Calories 320 (Calories from Fat 150);
Total Fat 17g (Saturated Fat 5g);
Cholesterol 85mg; Sodium 900mg;
Total Carbohydrates 33g (Dietary
Fiber 3g); Sugars 3g; Protein 12g

% Daily Value: Vitamin A 10%;
Vitamin C 10%; Calcium 15%; Iron 8%

Exchanges: 2 Starch, 1 High-Fat Meat,
1 1/2 Fat

Carbohydrate Choices: 2

QUICK FIX

If fresh cilantro isn't available, you can use 1/4 cup fresh chopped or 1 tablespoon
dried basil instead.

Ravioli with Corn and Cilantro

Three-Pepper Pasta with Pesto
Peas with Dill
Caesar Salad
Crusty French Rolls

4 servings

1. Cook the ziti.
2. While the ziti cooks, make the peas.
3. Make a purchased bag of Caesar salad.
4. Make the three-pepper pasta with pesto.

Peas with Dill

1 teaspoon butter or margarine
1/4 cup chopped onion
1 package (16 oz.) frozen sweet peas
2 tablespoons diced roasted red pepper or pimiento, drained
1 teaspoon dried dill

1. In medium nonstick skillet, melt butter over low heat. Add onion; cook and stir until tender.
2. Stir in remaining ingredients; cook 8 to 10 minutes or until thoroughly heated.

1 SERVING
Calories 80 (Calories from Fat 10);
Total Fat 1g (Saturated Fat 0g);
Cholesterol 0mg; Sodium 100mg;
Total Carbohydrates 16g (Dietary Fiber 6g); Sugars 6g; Protein 5g
% Daily Value: Vitamin A 20%;
Vitamin C 15%; Calcium 4%; Iron 10%
Exchanges: 1 Starch
Carbohydrate Choices: 1/2

QUICK FIX

The peas can be cooked in the microwave. In 1-quart microwave-safe casserole, microwave butter on High for 20 seconds until melted. Add onion. Microwave on High for 1 to 2 minutes or until tender. Stir in remaining ingredients. Microwave on High for 3 to 4 minutes or until thoroughly heated, stirring once halfway through cooking.

Three-Pepper Pasta with Pesto

2 1/4 cups uncooked ziti pasta (8 oz.)
1 tablespoon olive or vegetable oil
1 medium onion, cut into thin wedges
1 medium red or orange bell pepper, cut
    into bite-size strips
1 medium yellow bell pepper, cut into
    bite-size strips
1 small green bell pepper, cut into
    bite-size strips
1/3 cup basil pesto
2 teaspoons balsamic vinegar
1/4 cup shredded Asiago or Parmesan
    cheese (1 oz.)

1. Cook ziti as directed on package. Drain.
2. Meanwhile, in 12-inch skillet, heat oil over medium-high heat until hot. Add onion; cook and stir 2 minutes. Add bell peppers; cook 3 to 5 minutes or until onion and peppers are crisp-tender, stirring frequently.
3. Add cooked ziti; stir gently to mix. Remove from heat; stir in pesto and vinegar. If desired, add salt and pepper to taste. Sprinkle with cheese.

1 SERVING

Calories 400 (Calories from Fat 140);
Total Fat 16g (Saturated Fat 3g);
Cholesterol 10mg; Sodium 270mg;
Total Carbohydrates 50g (Dietary
Fiber 3g); Sugars 6g; Protein 13g

% Daily Value: Vitamin A 25%;
Vitamin C 90%; Calcium 15%; Iron 15%

Exchanges: 3 Starch, 1 Vegetable, 1/2 Lean
Meat, 2 1/2 Fat

Carbohydrate Choices: 3

QUICK FIX

If balsamic vinegar isn't a staple in your pantry, use 2 teaspoons cider vinegar and a pinch of brown sugar instead.

Pesto Shrimp and Pasta

Ready in 20 minutes

4 servings (1 cup each)

2 cups uncooked rotini pasta (6 oz.)
2 cups frozen broccoli florets, carrots and cauliflower
  (from 1-lb. bag)
8 oz. cooked peeled deveined small or medium shrimp,
  tails removed
1 container (7 oz.) refrigerated basil pesto (3/4 cup)
1/4 cup shredded Parmesan cheese (1 oz.)

1 In 2 1/2- to 3-quart saucepan, cook rotini as directed on
package, adding vegetables during last 5 minutes of cooking
time. Drain; return to saucepan.

2 Add shrimp and pesto; toss gently to coat. Sprinkle with
cheese.

1 SERVING

Calories 530 (Calories from Fat 270);
Total Fat 30g (Saturated Fat 7g);
Cholesterol 125mg; Sodium 880mg;
Total Carbohydrates 39g (Dietary
Fiber 4g); Sugars 2g; Protein 26g

% Daily Value: Vitamin A 38%;
Vitamin C 16%; Calcium 34%; Iron 26%

Exchanges: 2 Starch, 1 Vegetable,
2 1/2 Very Lean Meat, 6 Fat

Carbohydrate Choices: 2 1/2

QUICK FIX For perfect "al dente" pasta, cook the minimum time specified on the package, then remove a
noodle with a slotted spoon, run it briefly under cold water and bite into it. It should be firm
but cooked through with no hard center and not be mushy.

Summer Vegetable Ravioli

■ ■ ■ ■ Ready in 25 minutes

4 servings (1 1/2 cups each)

1 package (9 oz.) refrigerated cheese ravioli
2 tablespoons olive or vegetable oil
1 small onion, coarsely chopped (1/3 cup)
1 garlic clove, minced, or 1/8 teaspoon garlic powder
2 small zucchini, cut in half lengthwise, sliced
1 1/2 cups frozen whole kernel corn (from 1-lb. bag)
1/2 cup vegetable or chicken broth
6 medium Italian plum tomatoes, coarsely chopped and seeded (2 cups)
2 tablespoons chopped fresh or 1 1/2 teaspoons dried basil
1/4 cup shredded Parmesan cheese (1 oz.)

1 Cook ravioli as directed on package. Drain; cover to keep warm.

2 Meanwhile, in 10-inch skillet, heat oil over medium-high heat until hot. Add onion and garlic; cook and stir 2 minutes. Stir in zucchini, corn and broth. Bring to a boil. Reduce heat; simmer 3 to 5 minutes or until zucchini is crisp-tender.

3 Add tomatoes, basil and cooked ravioli; cook 3 to 5 minutes or until thoroughly heated and slightly thickened, stirring occasionally. If desired, add salt and pepper to taste. Sprinkle with cheese.

1 SERVING

Calories 380 (Calories from Fat 150);
Total Fat 17g (Saturated Fat 6g);
Cholesterol 60mg; Sodium 490mg;
Total Carbohydrates 41g (Dietary
Fiber 4g); Sugars 7g; Protein 15g

% Daily Value: Vitamin A 15%;
Vitamin C 20%; Calcium 25%; Iron 10%

Exchanges: 2 1/2 Starch, 1 Vegetable,
1/2 Lean Meat, 3 Fat

Carbohydrate Choices: 3

QUICK FIX

Let the kids set the table, then save on cleanup time by serving the meal right from the skillet. Just place it on a hot pad or trivet in the center of the table and, voilá, it's dinner!

Four

Hot from the Grill

Superfast Ready in 15 minutes or less

Sweet-and-Sour Meatball Kabobs

■ ■ ■ ■ **Ready in 25 minutes**

4 servings

1 large green bell pepper, cut into 12 pieces
8 thin wedges red onion
12 small fresh mushrooms
1/2 teaspoon seasoned salt
16 frozen cooked meatballs, thawed
3/4 cup sweet-and-sour sauce

1 Heat gas or charcoal grill. In large bowl, combine bell pepper, onion and mushrooms. Sprinkle with seasoned salt; toss to coat.

2 Onto four 12- to 14-inch metal skewers, alternately thread meatballs, bell pepper, onion and mushrooms.

3 When grill is heated, place kabobs on gas grill over medium heat or on charcoal grill 4 to 6 inches from medium coals. Cook covered 10 to 15 minutes or until meatballs are thoroughly heated and vegetables are crisp-tender, brushing generously with half of the sweet-and-sour sauce and turning frequently. Heat remaining sweet-and-sour sauce to a boil; boil 1 minute. Serve sauce with kabobs for dipping.

1 SERVING

Calories 405 (Calories from Fat 190);
Total Fat 21g (Saturated Fat 8g);
Cholesterol 125mg; Sodium 1,000mg;
Total Carbohydrates 30g (Dietary
Fiber 2g); Sugars 14g; Protein 24g

% Daily Value: Vitamin A 8%;
Vitamin C 32%; Calcium 8%; Iron 22%

Exchanges: 1 Starch, 3 Medium-Fat Meat,
1 Fat, 1 Other Carbohydrate

Carbohydrate Choices: 2

Broiled Sweet-and-Sour Meatball Kabobs: Place kabobs on broiler pan; broil 4 to 6 inches from heat using times above as a guide, brushing generously with half of the sweet-and-sour sauce and turning frequently.

QUICK FIX

Thaw the meatballs quickly in the microwave, about 4 to 6 minutes on Defrost ought to do the trick!

Juicy Burgers

4 sandwiches

1 egg
1 lb. lean (at least 80%) ground beef
1/4 cup Italian-style dry bread crumbs
1/4 cup milk
1 teaspoon dried instant minced onion
1/2 teaspoon salt
1/8 teaspoon pepper
4 burger buns, split

1. Heat gas or charcoal grill. In large bowl, beat egg. Stir in all remaining ingredients except buns until well mixed. Shape mixture into 4 (1/2-inch-thick) patties.

2. When grill is heated, place patties on gas grill over medium heat or on charcoal grill 4 to 6 inches from medium coals. Cook covered 11 to 13 minutes or until meat thermometer inserted in center of patties reads 160°F, turning once.

3. If desired, to toast buns, during last minute of cooking time, place buns, cut sides down, on grill. Serve patties in toasted buns with desired condiments.

Broiled Juicy Burgers: Place patties on broiler pan; broil 4 to 6 inches from heat using times above as a guide, turning once. To toast buns, during last 1 to 2 minutes of cooking time, place buns, cut sides up, on broiler pan.

1 SANDWICH

Calories **400 (Calories from Fat 180);
Total Fat 20g (Saturated Fat 8g);
Cholesterol 120mg; Sodium 670mg;
Total Carbohydrates 28g (Dietary
Fiber 1g); Sugars 7g; Protein 27g**

% Daily Value: **Vitamin A 4%;
Vitamin C 0%; Calcium 10%; Iron 20%**

Exchanges: **2 Starch, 3 Medium-Fat Meat,
1 Fat**

Carbohydrate Choices: **2**

QUICK FIX

For the perfect outdoor picnic, pick up potato salad at the deli and grill some fresh corn on the cob next to the burgers. Save on dishes by serving the meal on colorful disposable plates.

Juicy Burgers

Marinated Mushroom-Topped Burgers
Fresh Tomato and Lettuce Salad
Pickles and Olives
S'mores Nachos

4 servings

1 Heat the grill. Shape and cook the ground beef patties.

2 While the patties cook, slice two tomatoes and arrange on bibb lettuce or mixed salad greens. Serve with favorite salad dressing.

3 Toast rolls and make the burgers; serve with pickles and olives.

4 For dessert, heat the broiler. Make the s'mores nachos.

S'mores Nachos

8 rectangular graham crackers
3/4 cup milk chocolate chips
1 1/2 cups miniature marshmallows

1 Break each graham cracker into 4 pieces. Pile pieces in ungreased metal or disposable foil pie pan. DO NOT USE GLASS. Top with chocolate chips and marshmallows.

2 Broil 6 inches from heat for 30 to 60 seconds or until marshmallows are puffed and golden, watching to prevent burning.

1 SERVING
Calories 340 (Calories from Fat 110); Total Fat 12g (Saturated Fat 6g); Cholesterol 5mg; Sodium 190mg; Total Carbohydrates 55g (Dietary Fiber 1g); Sugars 40g; Protein 4g
% Daily Value: Vitamin A 0%; Vitamin C 0%; Calcium 6%; Iron 6%
Exchanges: 1 Starch, 2 1/2 Fat, 2 1/2 Other Carbohydrates
Carbohydrate Choices: 3 1/2

QUICK FIX

The popular campfire s'mores use chocolate but for a flavor twist use butterscotch or peanut butter chips rather than the milk chocolate chips. Kids of all ages will love them!

Marinated Mushroom—Topped Burgers

1 lb. lean (at least 80%) ground beef
1 1/2 teaspoons lemon-pepper seasoning
2 cups sliced fresh mushrooms (about 5 oz.)
1/4 cup balsamic vinaigrette
4 kaiser rolls, split
4 (1-oz.) slices Swiss cheese

1. Heat gas or charcoal grill. In medium bowl, combine ground beef and 1 teaspoon of the lemon-pepper seasoning; mix well. Shape mixture into 4 (1/2-inch-thick) patties.

2. In another medium bowl, combine mushrooms, remaining 1/2 teaspoon lemon-pepper seasoning and vinaigrette; toss to coat. Set aside.

3. When grill is heated, place patties on gas grill over medium heat or on charcoal grill 4 to 6 inches from medium coals. Cook 11 to 13 minutes or until meat thermometer inserted in center of patties reads 160°F, turning once.

4. To toast rolls, during last 1 to 2 minutes of cooking time, place rolls, cut sides down, on grill. Place 1 slice of cheese on each patty; cook an additional minute or until cheese is melted.

5. Place patties on bottom halves of rolls. Top each with mushroom mixture and top half of roll.

Broiled Marinated Mushroom—Topped Burgers: Place patties on broiler pan; broil 4 to 6 inches from heat using times above as a guide, turning once. To toast rolls, during last 1 to 2 minutes of cooking time, place rolls, cut sides up, on broiler pan. Place 1 slice of cheese on each patty; cook an additional minute.

1 SANDWICH
Calories 555 (Calories from Fat 295);
Total Fat 33g (Saturated Fat 13g);
Cholesterol 90mg; Sodium 1,060mg;
Total Carbohydrates 29g (Dietary
Fiber 1g); Sugars 1g; Protein 35g
% Daily Value: Vitamin A 6%;
Vitamin C 0%; Calcium 32%; Iron 22%
Exchanges: 2 Starch, 4 Medium-Fat Meat,
2 1/2 Fat
Carbohydrate Choices: 2

QUICK FIX

Mushroom slicing is a thing of the past! Just look for packages of presliced mushrooms next to the whole mushrooms in the produce department. They're a great recipe time-saver!

Blue Cheese Burgers

4 sandwiches

1 lb. lean (at least 80%) ground beef
1/2 cup crumbled blue cheese (2 oz.)
1 teaspoon garlic-pepper blend
1/2 teaspoon salt
4 onion buns, split
4 tomato slices

1. Heat gas or charcoal grill. In medium bowl, combine all ingredients except buns and tomato slices; mix well. Shape mixture into 4 (1/2-inch-thick) patties.

2. When grill is heated, place patties on gas grill over medium heat or on charcoal grill 4 to 6 inches from medium coals. Cook 11 to 13 minutes or until meat thermometer inserted in center of patties reads 160°F, turning once.

3. If desired, to toast buns, during last 1 to 2 minutes of cooking time, place buns, cut sides down, on grill.

4. Place patties on bottom halves of buns. Top each with tomato slice. If desired, top with additional blue cheese. Cover with top halves of buns.

Broiled Blue Cheese Burgers: Place patties on broiler pan; broil 4 to 6 inches from heat using times above as a guide, turning once. To toast buns, during last 1 to 2 minutes of cooking time, place buns, cut sides up, on broiler pan.

1 SANDWICH

Calories 390 (Calories from Fat 190); Total Fat 21g (Saturated Fat 9g); Cholesterol 80mg; Sodium 860mg; Total Carbohydrates 23g (Dietary Fiber 1g); Sugars 6g; Protein 27g

% Daily Value: Vitamin A 4%; Vitamin C 2%; Calcium 15%; Iron 20%

Exchanges: 1 1/2 Starch, 3 Medium-Fat Meat, 1 Fat

Carbohydrate Choices: 1 1/2

QUICK FIX

Get your charcoal grill going in a flash! Look for charcoal starter cubes where you find grilling supplies. These compact squares will burn for 5 to 10 minutes and help get coals burning in a minimum amount of time.

Onion-Topped Burgers

■ ■ ■ ■ **Ready in 25 minutes**

4 sandwiches

Photo on page 109

1 lb. lean (at least 80%) ground beef
1/4 cup fresh bread crumbs
1/4 cup beef broth or water
2 tablespoons dry French onion soup mix (from 1-oz. package)
1 large sweet onion (Walla Walla, Maui or Texas Sweet), cut into
    1/8-inch-thick slices, separated into rings
2 tablespoons beef broth or water
1/4 teaspoon salt
1/4 teaspoon pepper
4 burger buns, split

1. Heat gas or charcoal grill. In medium bowl, combine ground beef, bread crumbs, 1/4 cup beef broth and soup mix; mix well. Shape mixture into 4 (1/2-inch-thick) patties. Place sliced onion, 2 tablespoons beef broth, salt and pepper in foil grilling bag or foil packet.
2. When grill is heated, place patties and grilling bag with onion mixture on gas grill over medium heat or on charcoal grill 4 to 6 inches from medium coals. Cook 11 to 13 minutes or until meat thermometer inserted in center of patties reads 160°F, turning patties once and turning grilling bag frequently.
3. To toast buns, during last 1 to 2 minutes of cooking time, place buns, cut side down, on grill.
4. Place patties on bottom halves of buns. Top each with onions and top half of bun.

1 SANDWICH

Calories 370 (Calories from Fat 150);
**Total Fat 17g (Saturated Fat 6g);
Cholesterol 70mg; Sodium 830mg;
Total Carbohydrates 30g (Dietary
Fiber 3g); Sugars 9g; Protein 25g**

% Daily Value: **Vitamin A 0%;
Vitamin C 4%; Calcium 8%; Iron 20%**

Exchanges: **2 Starch, 3 Medium-Fat Meat**

Carbohydrate Choices: **2**

QUICK FIX

Water adds moistness to these grilled burgers. If you prefer, use 1/4 cup of tomato juice—or for an adult cookout, dark beer—instead of beef broth.

Bistro Burgers

■ ■ ■ ■ **Ready in 25 minutes**

4 sandwiches

1 1/2 lb. lean (at least 80%) ground beef
1/4 teaspoon salt
1/4 teaspoon pepper
4 kaiser rolls, split
1/4 cup creamy mustard-mayonnaise sauce
4 thin slices sweet onion (Walla Walla, Maui or Texas Sweet)
4 tomato slices
4 oz. thinly sliced fresh Parmesan cheese
1/2 cup fresh basil leaves

1. Heat gas or charcoal grill. In medium bowl, combine ground beef, salt and pepper; mix well. Shape mixture into 4 (1/2-inch-thick) patties.

2. When grill is heated, place patties on gas grill over medium heat or on charcoal grill 4 to 6 inches from medium coals. Cook covered 11 to 13 minutes or until meat thermometer inserted in center of patties reads 160°F, turning once.

3. To toast rolls, during last 1 to 2 minutes of cooking time, place rolls, cut sides down, on grill.

4. Spread cut sides of rolls with mustard-mayonnaise sauce. Place patties on bottom halves of rolls. Top each with onion, tomato, cheese, basil and top half of roll.

1 SANDWICH

Calories 640 (Calories from Fat 320); Total Fat 35g (Saturated Fat 15g); Cholesterol 125mg; Sodium 1,160mg; Total Carbohydrates 35g (Dietary Fiber 2g); Sugars 2g; Protein 46g

% Daily Value: Vitamin A 8%; Vitamin C 4%; Calcium 40%; Iron 25%

Exchanges: 2 Starch, 5 1/2 Medium-Fat Meat, 1 Fat

Carbohydrate Choices: 2

Broiled Bistro Burgers: Place patties on broiler pan; broil 4 to 6 inches from heat using times above as a guide, turning once. To toast rolls, during last 1 to 2 minutes of cooking time, place rolls, cut side up, on broiler pan.

QUICK FIX

Double up on the amount of ground beef patty ingredients, then make 4 extra patties for the freezer. Wrap each patty individually in plastic wrap, and store them in a resealable plastic freezer bag. When it's time to grill again, just thaw the patties in the refrigerator and grill as directed.

Bistro Burgers

Steaks with Lemon-Chive Butter
Grilled Zucchini
Grilled Pesto French Bread
Raspberry Sherbet

4 servings

1 Heat the grill. Make the lemon-chive butter and the cream cheese mixture for the bread.

2 Slice 2 medium zucchini into 1/2-inch slices. Toss with olive oil; place in grilling basket and sprinkle with salt and pepper.

3 Season steaks with pepper mixture and grill. Add the bread to the grill.

4 When steaks are almost done, add zucchini to the grill and cook 2 to 3 minutes or until tender.

Grilled Pesto French Bread

1/4 cup butter or margarine, softened
1 package (3 oz.) cream cheese, softened
1/2 cup basil pesto
1 loaf (1 lb.) French bread, halved crosswise, split lengthwise

1 Heat gas or charcoal grill. In small bowl, mix butter, cream cheese and pesto.

2 When grill is heated, place bread pieces, cut sides down, on gas grill over medium heat or on charcoal grill 4 to 6 inches from medium coals. Cook covered 1 to 2 minutes or until lightly brown.

3 Turn bread pieces over; spread pesto mixture evenly on cut sides of bread. Cook covered 3 to 4 minutes or until heated. Cut bread into 2-inch sections.

Broiled Pesto French Bread: Place bread, cut sides up, on broiler pan. Broil 4 or 5 inches from heat using times above as a guide. Spread pesto on bread as directed above.

1 SERVING

Calories **160** (Calories from Fat 90);
Total Fat 10g (Saturated Fat 4g);
**Cholesterol 15mg; Sodium 270mg;
Total Carbohydrates 15g** (Dietary
Fiber 0g); **Sugars 0g; Protein 4g**

% Daily Value: **Vitamin A 4%;
Vitamin C 0%; Calcium 6%; Iron 6%**

Exchanges: **1 Starch, 2 Fat**

Carbohydrate Choices: **1**

QUICK FIX

There are other flavors of pesto available, so the next time you are in the store pick up a jar of sun-dried tomato pesto for a nice flavor change.

Steaks with Lemon-Chive Butter

Butter

3 tablespoons butter or margarine, softened
2 teaspoons chopped fresh or
   3/4 teaspoon dried chives
1/2 teaspoon grated lemon peel
1 teaspoon lemon juice

Steaks

2 teaspoons coarse ground pepper
1/2 teaspoon garlic salt
4 (1-inch-thick) beef top loin steaks
   (New York, Kansas City or strip
   steaks)

1 Heat gas or charcoal grill. In small bowl, combine all butter ingredients; blend well. Set aside.

2 In another small bowl, combine pepper and garlic salt; mix well. Rub pepper mixture onto all surfaces of steaks.

3 When grill is heated, place steaks on gas grill over medium-high heat or on charcoal grill 4 to 6 inches from medium-high coals. Cook covered 8 to 12 minutes or until of desired doneness, turning once. Serve steaks with butter.

Broiled Steaks with Lemon-Chive Butter: Place steaks on broiler pan; broil 4 to 6 inches from heat using times above as a guide, turning once.

1 SERVING

Calories 430 (Calories from Fat 150);
Total Fat 17g (Saturated Fat 11g);
Cholesterol 150mg; Sodium 290mg;
Total Carbohydrates 1g (Dietary Fiber 0g);
Sugars 0g; Protein 47g

% Daily Value: Vitamin A 14%;
Vitamin C 0%; Calcium 2%; Iron 24%

Exchanges: 6 1/2 Lean Meat, 1 Fat

Carbohydrate Choices: 0

QUICK FIX
If you are pressed for time and the butter is not softened, there's no need to wait! Just microwave the butter in a small microwavable dish on Low or Defrost for 20 to 30 seconds or until soft.

Open-Faced Italian Steak Sandwiches Superfast

4 sandwiches

2 tablespoons butter or margarine, softened
1 tablespoon basil pesto
1 tablespoon sun-dried tomato spread
1 (1-lb.) boneless beef sirloin steak (about 1/2 inch thick),
    cut into 4 pieces
Dash salt and pepper
4 slices frozen garlic Texas toast

1. Heat gas or charcoal grill. In small bowl, combine butter, pesto and tomato spread; blend well. Set aside.

2. When grill is heated, sprinkle steaks with salt and pepper; place steaks on gas grill over medium heat or on charcoal grill 4 to 6 inches from medium coals. Cook covered 5 to 8 minutes or until of desired doneness, turning once.

3. During last 3 minutes of cooking time, place Texas toast on grill; cook until golden brown, turning once.

4. Place Texas toast slices on individual serving plates. Top each with 1 steak and seasoned butter.

Broiled Open-Faced Italian Steak Sandwiches: Place steaks on broiler pan; broil 4 to 6 inches from heat using times above as a guide, turning once. During last 3 minutes of cooking time, place Texas toast on broiler pan; broil until golden brown, turning once.

1 SANDWICH

Calories 330 (Calories from Fat 155); Total Fat 17g (Saturated Fat 6g); Cholesterol 75mg; Sodium 410mg; Total Carbohydrates 18g (Dietary Fiber 1g); Sugars 0g; Protein 26g

% Daily Value: Vitamin A 10%; Vitamin C 0%; Calcium 4%; Iron 18%

Exchanges: 1 Starch, 3 1/2 Lean Meat, 1 1/2 Fat

Carbohydrate Choices: 1

QUICK FIX

Get rid of the grit on the grill rack quickly. Just heat the rack on the grill prior to cooking, then brush the hot rack (while it's in place) with a wire grill brush or a wad of crumpled aluminum foil, and voilá, it's clean!

Open-Faced Italian Steak Sandwiches

Pesto-Stuffed Tenderloins

■ ■ ■ ■ **Ready in 20 minutes**

4 servings

4 (1-inch-thick) beef tenderloin steaks (about 3/4 lb.)
4 tablespoons basil pesto
2 teaspoons vegetable oil
1/2 teaspoon salt
1/4 to 1/2 teaspoon pepper

1 Heat gas or charcoal grill. With narrow sharp knife, make 1-inch slit in one side of each steak. Make pocket in each steak by moving knife around inside of steak. (Do not enlarge 1-inch opening because pesto will come out during cooking.)

2 Spoon 1 tablespoon pesto into each steak, spreading pesto around inside of steak. Brush all sides of steaks with oil; sprinkle with salt and pepper.

3 When grill is heated, place steaks on gas grill over medium heat or on charcoal grill 4 to 6 inches from medium coals. Cook covered 7 to 11 minutes or until of desired doneness, turning once.

Broiled Pesto-Stuffed Tenderloins: Place stuffed steaks on broiler pan; broil 4 to 6 inches from heat using times above as a guide, turning once.

1 SERVING

Calories 235 (Calories from Fat 155); Total Fat 17g (Saturated Fat 4g); Cholesterol 50mg; Sodium 480mg; Total Carbohydrates 1g (Dietary Fiber 0g); Sugars 0g; Protein 20g

% Daily Value: Vitamin A 4%; Vitamin C 0%; Calcium 6%; Iron 10%

Exchanges: 3 Lean Meat, 1 1/2 Fat

Carbohydrate Choices: 0

QUICK FIX

For easy grilling and to prevent lean cuts of meat, such as beef tenderloin, from sticking to the grill, scrape the hot rack clean of cooked-on particles and brush the meat with just a bit of oil before placing it on the grill.

Steaks with Blue Cheese Butter

■ ■ ■ ■ **Ready in 25 minutes**   *4 servings*

Butter

1/4 cup butter or margarine, softened
1/4 cup crumbled blue cheese (1 oz.)
2 teaspoons chopped fresh or 3/4 teaspoon dried chives

Steaks

4 (1 1/2-inch-thick) beef tenderloin steaks (6 oz. each)
2 teaspoons garlic-pepper blend

1 Heat gas or charcoal grill. In small bowl, combine all butter
   ingredients; mix well.

2 When grill is heated, carefully oil grill rack. Sprinkle each
   steak with garlic-pepper blend. Place steaks on gas grill over
   medium heat or on charcoal grill 4 to 6 inches from medium
   coals. Cook covered 12 to 15 minutes or until of desired
   doneness, turning once or twice. Serve steaks with blue
   cheese butter.

Broiled Steaks with Blue Cheese Butter: Place steaks on broiler
pan; broil 4 to 6 inches from heat using times above as a guide, turning once
or twice.

1 SERVING

Calories 390 (Calories from Fat 235);
Total Fat 26g (Saturated Fat 13g);
Cholesterol 135mg; Sodium 260mg;
Total Carbohydrates 1g (Dietary Fiber 0g);
Sugars 0g; Protein 38g

% Daily Value: Vitamin A 12%;
Vitamin C 0%; Calcium 4%; Iron 18%

Exchanges: 5 1/2 Lean Meat, 2 Fat

Carbohydrate Choices: 0

QUICK FIX

A BBQ fork with built-in thermometer takes away the guesswork of checking to see if
meats and poultry are cooked sufficiently. The fork is battery-operated and available at
discount and kitchen specialty shops.

Individual Pepperoni Pizzas

■ ■ ■ ■ **Ready in 20 minutes**   *4 pizzas*

4 flour tortillas (8 inch)
2 teaspoons olive oil
1 1/2 cups finely shredded Cheddar and
    Monterey Jack cheese blend (6 oz.)
1/2 cup sliced pimiento-stuffed green olives
1/2 cup diced tomato, well drained
24 slices (1 inch) pepperoni
1 teaspoon dried oregano leaves

1. Heat gas or charcoal grill. Place tortillas on ungreased cookie sheets. Brush with oil. Sprinkle with 1 cup of the cheese. Top evenly with olives, tomato and pepperoni. Sprinkle with remaining cheese and oregano.

2. When grill is heated, with broad spatula, carefully slide pizzas onto gas grill over medium heat or onto charcoal grill 4 to 6 inches from medium coals. Cook covered 3 to 6 minutes or until cheese is melted and crust is crisp. To remove from grill, slide pizzas back onto cookie sheets.

1 PIZZA
Calories 515 (Calories from Fat 325);
Total Fat 36g (Saturated Fat 15g);
Cholesterol 70mg; Sodium 1,590mg;
Total Carbohydrates 27g (Dietary
Fiber 1g); Sugars 3g; Protein 21g

% Daily Value: Vitamin A 14%;
Vitamin C 2%; Calcium 34%; Iron 14%

Exchanges: 2 Starch, 2 High-Fat Meat, 4 Fat

Carbohydrate Choices: 2

QUICK FIX

Assemble these tasty pizzas on a large rimless cookie sheet, and they will slide easily on and off the hot grill. If all of your cookie sheets have rims, simply turn one upside down and assemble the pizzas on the underside. This tricky technique not only helps transfer the pizzas easily but also keeps them conveniently all together.

Individual
Pepper Pizzas

Kielbasa-Vegetable Kabobs
Romaine-Broccoli Salad with Strawberries
Sourdough Rolls
Brownie Banana Splits

4 servings

1. Bake a box of brownies or use purchased brownies.
2. Make the kabobs and cook on grill.
3. While kabobs cook, make the salad.
4. For dessert, cut 2 bananas crosswise in half. Cut each half lengthwise in half to make 8 pieces.
5. Place 2 banana pieces in each bowl. Top with a brownie and a scoop of vanilla ice cream. Drizzle with chocolate sauce and sprinkle with nuts.

Romaine-Broccoli Salad with Strawberries

4 cups torn romaine lettuce
2 cups broccoli-coleslaw blend (from 16-oz. package)
1 cup fresh strawberries, quartered
2 thin slices red onion, quartered
1/3 cup raspberry vinaigrette salad dressing

1. In large serving bowl, combine all ingredients except salad dressing; toss to mix.
2. Pour dressing over salad; toss to coat.

1 SERVING

Calories 75 (Calories from Fat 45);
Total Fat 5g (Saturated Fat 1g);
Cholesterol 0mg; Sodium 40mg;
Total Carbohydrates 6g (Dietary Fiber 2g);
Sugars 5g; Protein 2g

% Daily Value: Vitamin A 24%;
Vitamin C 42%; Calcium 2%; Iron 4%

Exchanges: 1 Vegetable, 1 Fat

Carbohydrate Choices: 1/2

QUICK FIX

Broccoli-coleslaw blend is convenient to use in salads but if it isn't available you can still make this colorful salad by using 2 cups of small broccoli florets.

Kielbasa-Vegetable Kabobs

12 oz. cooked kielbasa, cut into
   1-inch pieces
2 cans (15 oz.) whole potatoes, drained, rinsed
   with cold water
16 cherry tomatoes
16 (1-inch) pieces zucchini
1/2 cup honey-mustard barbecue sauce

1. Heat gas or charcoal grill. Onto eight
   10- to 12-inch metal skewers, alternately
   thread all ingredients except barbecue sauce.
   Brush kabobs with barbecue sauce.
2. When grill is heated, place kabobs on gas grill
   over medium heat or on charcoal grill
   4 to 6 inches from medium coals. Cook covered
   5 to 8 minutes or until kielbasa is deep golden
   brown, turning frequently and brushing twice with
   barbecue sauce. If desired, serve with additional
   warm barbecue sauce.

Broiled Kielbasa-Vegetable Kabobs: Place kabobs on broiler pan;
broil 4 to 6 inches from heat using times above as a guide, turning frequently
and brushing twice with barbecue sauce.

1 SERVING

Calories 450 (Calories from Fat 215);
Total Fat 24g (Saturated Fat 9g);
Cholesterol 50mg; Sodium 2,090mg;
Total Carbohydrates 44g (Dietary
Fiber 7g); Sugars 12g; Protein 14g

% Daily Value: Vitamin A 26%;
Vitamin C 28%; Calcium 4%; Iron 22%

Exchanges: 2 Starch, 1 Vegetable,
1 High-Fat Meat, 3 1/2 Fat

Carbohydrate Choices: 2 1/2

QUICK FIX

Want to save time by turning all of your kabobs at once? Just invest in a
two-sided hinged grill basket. You can conveniently place all 8 kabobs
between the basket sides, then it's a cinch to simply turn the whole thing
with the long handle.

Salsa Hot Dog Wraps *Superfast*

■ ■ ■ Ready in 15 minutes

4 sandwiches

4 flour tortillas (8 inch)
4 hot dogs
1/2 cup chunky salsa
1/2 cup shredded lettuce
2 (1-oz.) slices mild Cheddar cheese, halved

1. Heat gas or charcoal grill. Wrap tortillas securely in heavy-duty foil.
2. When grill is heated, place hot dogs and tortilla packet on gas grill over medium heat or on charcoal grill 4 to 6 inches from medium coals. Cook covered 5 to 10 minutes or until hot dogs and tortillas are thoroughly heated, turning hot dogs frequently and turning tortilla packet once halfway through cooking time.
3. On each warm tortilla, layer salsa, lettuce, hot dog and cheese. Fold in 2 sides of each tortilla; roll up.

1 SANDWICH

Calories 355 (Calories from Fat 190);
Total Fat 21g (Saturated Fat 9g);
Cholesterol 40mg; Sodium 970mg;
Total Carbohydrates 28g (Dietary
Fiber 2g); Sugars 3g; Protein 13g

% Daily Value: Vitamin A 8%;
Vitamin C 4%; Calcium 14%; Iron 12%

Exchanges: 2 Starch, 1 High-Fat Meat,
2 1/2 Fat

Carbohydrate Choices: 2

QUICK FIX

Make this kid-favorite sandwich even when the weather isn't great for grilling. Just heat the hot dogs as directed on the package. Stack the tortillas on a microwave-safe plate, cover with microwavable plastic wrap and microwave on High for 1 minute.

Taco Pork Chops

■ ■ ■ ■ Ready in 20 minutes   *4 servings*

1 package (1.25 oz.) taco seasoning mix
2 tablespoons lime juice
1 tablespoon honey
4 (1/2-inch-thick) boneless pork loin chops (4 oz. each)
1 ripe medium avocado, pitted, peeled and cut up
1 tablespoon chopped fresh cilantro, if desired

1. Heat gas or charcoal grill. Reserve 2 teaspoons taco seasoning mix for topping. In small bowl, combine remaining taco seasoning mix, 1 tablespoon of the lime juice and the honey; mix well. Brush mixture on both sides of each pork chop. Discard any remaining mixture.

2. When grill is heated, place pork chops on gas grill over medium heat or on charcoal grill 4 to 6 inches from medium coals. Cook covered 8 to 10 minutes or until pork is slightly pink in center, turning once or twice.

3. Meanwhile, in small bowl, combine avocado, reserved 2 teaspoons taco seasoning mix and remaining 1 tablespoon lime juice; mash with fork until almost smooth.

4. Serve pork chops topped with avocado mixture. Sprinkle with cilantro.

Broiled Taco Pork Chops: Place pork chops on broiler pan; broil 4 to 6 inches from heat using times above as a guide, turning once or twice.

1 SERVING
Calories 300 (Calories from Fat 140); Total Fat 16g (Saturated Fat 4g); Cholesterol 70mg; Sodium 870mg; Total Carbohydrates 14g (Dietary Fiber 3g); Sugars 5g; Protein 26g
% Daily Value: Vitamin A 10%; Vitamin C 8%; Calcium 4%; Iron 15%
Exchanges: 1 Starch, 3 1/2 Lean Meat, 1 Fat
Carbohydrate Choices: 1

QUICK FIX
Use a disposable plate or waxed paper when you prepare the pork chops for the grill. Then, for food safety, be sure to use a clean plate to serve the chops.

Honey-Glazed Pork Chops

■ ■ ■ ■ **Ready in 25 minutes**   *4 servings*

Glaze
2 tablespoons ketchup
2 tablespoons honey
2 tablespoons white wine vinegar
1 teaspoon dried thyme leaves
1/2 teaspoon ground mustard
2 garlic cloves, minced, or 1/4 teaspoon garlic powder

Pork Chops
1 teaspoon paprika
1/2 teaspoon peppered seasoned salt
4 (6- to 7-oz. each) bone-in pork loin chops

1. Heat gas or charcoal grill. In small microwavable bowl, combine all glaze ingredients; mix well. Microwave on High for 30 seconds. Stir; set aside.

2. In small bowl, combine paprika and peppered seasoned salt. Sprinkle both sides of pork chops with paprika mixture; rub into surface of pork.

3. When grill is heated, place pork on gas grill over medium heat or on charcoal grill 4 to 6 inches from medium coals. Cook covered 12 to 15 minutes or until pork is slightly pink when cut near bone, turning twice, and brushing glaze on each side during last 5 minutes of cooking time. Discard any remaining glaze.

Broiled Honey-Glazed Pork Chops: Place pork chops on broiler pan; broil 4 to 6 inches from heat using times above as a guide, turning twice, and brushing glaze on each side during last 2 minutes of cooking time.

1 SERVING

Calories 230 (Calories from Fat 90);
Total Fat 10g (Saturated Fat 4g);
Cholesterol 85mg; Sodium 140mg;
Total Carbohydrates 3g (Dietary Fiber 0g);
Sugars 2g; Protein 31g

% Daily Value: Vitamin A 6%;
Vitamin C 0%; Calcium 2%; Iron 8%

Exchanges: 4 1/2 Lean Meat

Carbohydrate Choices: 0

QUICK FIX

Avoid all of that running back and forth from the kitchen to the grill by outfitting yourself with a tool with all the essentials you're likely to need at the grill. Choose a wicker, plastic or wire basket that your tools will fit in, and keep it ready to go for grill nights!

Honey-Glazed Pork Chops

Ham and Pineapple Kabobs

■ ■ ■ **Ready in 20 minutes**   *4 servings*

1 lb. cooked ham, cut into 1-inch cubes
1 can (8 oz.) pineapple chunks in unsweetened juice, drained
8 cherry tomatoes
3/4 cup red currant or apple jelly
1 tablespoon prepared yellow mustard

1. Heat gas or charcoal grill. Onto four 10-inch metal skewers, alternately thread ham, pineapple and tomatoes.

2. In small microwavable bowl, combine jelly and mustard; mix well. Microwave on High for 1 to 2 minutes or until jelly melts. Stir to combine. Brush 3 to 4 tablespoons jelly mixture over kabobs.

3. When grill is heated, place kabobs on gas grill over medium heat or on charcoal grill 4 to 6 inches from medium coals. Cook covered 10 to 12 minutes or until thoroughly heated, turning once. Serve with remaining jelly mixture.

Broiled Ham and Pineapple Kabobs: Place kabobs on broiler pan; broil 4 to 6 inches from heat using times above as a guide, turning once.

1 SERVING
Calories 405 (Calories from Fat 100); Total Fat 11g (Saturated Fat 4g); Cholesterol 65mg; Sodium 1,770mg; Total Carbohydrates 50g (Dietary Fiber 1g); Sugars 37g; Protein 27g

% Daily Value: Vitamin A 6%; Vitamin C 14%; Calcium 2%; Iron 12%

Exchanges: 4 Lean Meat, 3 Other Carbohydrates

Carbohydrate Choices: 3

QUICK FIX

Ham from the deli or leftover from Sunday dinner can be used for these kabobs. At the deli, ask for 1-inch slices to cube for the kabobs.

Lamb Chops with Orange Butter

■ ■ ■ ■ Ready in 20 minutes

4 servings

Butter
1/4 cup butter or margarine, softened
1 tablespoon chopped fresh parsley
4 teaspoons grated orange peel
1 teaspoon ground coriander, if desired

Lamb Chops
8 (3-oz. each) lamb loin chops
2 tablespoons olive oil
1/2 teaspoon salt
1/2 teaspoon pepper

1. Heat gas or charcoal grill. In small bowl, combine all butter ingredients; blend well. Place butter mixture on sheet of plastic wrap; shape into log. Wrap; refrigerate while preparing chops.

2. When grill is heated, rub both sides of lamb chops with oil; sprinkle with salt and pepper. Place chops on gas grill over medium heat or on charcoal grill 4 to 6 inches from medium coals. Cook covered 7 to 10 minutes or until of desired doneness, turning once or twice.

3. Top each lamb chop with slice of orange butter.

Broiled Lamb Chops with Orange Butter: Place lamb chops on broiler pan; broil 4 to 6 inches from heat using times above as a guide, turning once or twice.

1 SERVING
Calories 295 (Calories from Fat 215);
Total Fat 24g (Saturated Fat 10g);
Cholesterol 95mg; Sodium 420mg;
Total Carbohydrates 1g (Dietary Fiber 0g);
Sugars 0g; Protein 19g
% Daily Value: Vitamin A 12%;
Vitamin C 4%; Calcium 2%; Iron 10%
Exchanges: 2 1/2 Lean Meat, 3 1/2 Fat
Carbohydrate Choices: 0

QUICK FIX

Make the easy butter topping for these lamb chops right before you grill them, or mix it up and wrap in plastic wrap to store in the refrigerator for up to 1 week. This tasty butter is also great on grilled pork or chicken.

Barbecue Chipotle Chicken

■ ■ ■ ■ **Ready in 25 minutes**   *4 servings*

1/2 cup barbecue sauce
2 tablespoons finely chopped onion
1 tablespoon chopped chipotle chilies in adobo sauce
4 boneless skinless chicken breast halves

1. Heat gas or charcoal grill. In 1-quart saucepan, combine barbecue sauce, onion and chiles; mix well.

2. When grill is heated, lightly brush sauce mixture on one side of each chicken breast half. Place chicken, sauce side down, on gas grill over medium heat or on charcoal grill 4 to 6 inches from medium coals. Lightly brush sauce over chicken. Cook covered 10 to 16 minutes or until juice is clear when center of thickest part is cut (170°F).

3. Heat remaining sauce to a boil; boil 1 minute. Serve chicken with sauce.

Broiled Barbecue Chipotle Chicken: Place chicken on broiler pan; lightly brush sauce mixture over top of each chicken breast half. Broil 4 to 6 inches from heat using times above as a guide, turning and brushing once with sauce mixture.

1 SERVING

Calories 190 (Calories from Fat 35); Total Fat 4g (Saturated Fat 1g); Cholesterol 75mg; Sodium 390mg; Total Carbohydrates 12g (Dietary Fiber 0g); Sugars 9g; Protein 27g

% Daily Value: Vitamin A 2%; Vitamin C 2%; Calcium 2%; Iron 6%

Exchanges: 1 Starch, 3 1/2 Very Lean Meat, 1/2 Fat

Carbohydrate Choices: 1

QUICK FIX

Extra chilis? Freeze any remaining chipotle chilies with the adobo sauce in small serving-size containers in the freezer for up to 3 months.

Wire cooling racks are made for cooling baked goods, but they also serve a variety of purposes that extend beyond your countertop.

1. Create an impromptu grill basket. Put oiled vegetables or seasoned fish fillets between two oiled cooling racks. Fasten the racks together with wire twist-ties. Use a spatula and an oven mitt–clad hand to flip the basket on the grill.

2. Use a cooling rack with a square grid to dice hard-cooked eggs for salads.

3. Need to increase shelf space in your fridge? Set cooling racks on top of food containers to give yourself more room.

4. Keep your countertop cool by using a wire rack as a trivet under your slow cooker.

5. When stovetop space is at a premium, place strips of bacon on a cooling rack and set the rack in a baking pan. Put the baking pan on the middle oven rack and cook the bacon in a 350° oven until crisp.

Apple-Honey-Mustard Chicken
Stuffing
Orange-Glazed Carrots and Sugar Snap Peas
Fresh Berries with Cream

4 servings

1 Heat the grill. Make glaze for chicken; cook chicken.

2 While chicken cooks, make the vegetables.

3 Make a box of chicken-flavored stuffing mix.

4 For dessert, pour whipping (heavy) cream or half-and-half over bowls of fresh berries. Sprinkle with brown sugar.

Orange-Glazed Carrots and Sugar Snap Peas

1 cup water
2 cups baby-cut carrots
1 cup frozen sugar snap peas (from 1-lb. bag)
2 tablespoons orange marmalade
1/4 teaspoon salt
Dash pepper

1 In 2-quart saucepan, heat water to boiling. Add carrots; return to boiling. Reduce heat to low; cover and simmer 8 to 10 minutes or until carrots are tender, adding sugar snap peas during last 5 minutes of cooking time. Drain; return to saucepan.

2 Stir in marmalade, salt and pepper. Cook and stir over medium heat until marmalade is melted and vegetables are glazed.

1 SERVING
Calories 45 (Calories from Fat 0); Total Fat 0g (Saturated Fat 0g); Cholesterol 0mg; Sodium 115mg; Total Carbohydrates 10g (Dietary Fiber 2g); Sugars 6g; Protein 1g
% Daily Value: Vitamin A 160%; Vitamin C 10%; Calcium 2%; Iron 4%
Exchanges: 1/2 Starch
Carbohydrate Choices: 1/2

QUICK FIX

If your family loves peas and carrots, try this orange-flavored veggie using 1 cup of frozen peas for the sugar snap peas.

Apple-Honey-Mustard Chicken

1 jar (12 oz.) apple jelly
1 teaspoon ground ginger
1/2 teaspoon garlic powder
2 tablespoons soy sauce
2 tablespoons honey
   mustard
4 boneless skinless
   chicken breast halves

1 Heat gas or charcoal grill. In 1-quart saucepan, combine all ingredients except chicken; mix well. Bring to a boil over medium heat. Boil 1 minute, stirring constantly.

2 When grill is heated, lightly brush glaze on one side of each chicken breast half. Place chicken, glaze side down, on gas grill over medium heat or on charcoal grill 4 to 6 inches from medium coals. Lightly brush glaze over chicken; cook covered 10 to 16 minutes or until juice is clear when center of thickest part is cut (170°F).

3 Heat remaining glaze to a boil; boil 1 minute. Serve chicken with glaze.

Broiled Apple-Honey-Mustard Chicken: Place chicken on broiler pan; broil 4 to 6 inches from heat using times above as a guide, turning once.

1 SERVING

Calories 355 (Calories from Fat 35); Total Fat 4g (Saturated Fat 1g); Cholesterol 75mg; Sodium 660mg; Total Carbohydrates 52g (Dietary Fiber 1g); Sugars 37g; Protein 28g

% Daily Value: Vitamin A 0%; Vitamin C 4%; Calcium 2%; Iron 8%

Exchanges: 4 Very Lean Meat, 3 1/2 Other Carbohydrates

Carbohydrate Choices: 3 1/2

QUICK FIX Forgot to pull the chicken breasts from the freezer? Frozen chicken breasts thaw quickly in the microwave on Defrost in 3 to 5 minutes.

Chicken Satay

■ ■ ■ Ready in 25 minutes

4 servings

2 tablespoons peanut butter
2 tablespoons teriyaki marinade and sauce
1/8 teaspoon crushed red pepper flakes
1 lb. boneless skinless chicken breast halves, cut into
     1/2-inch-thick strips

1 Heat gas or charcoal grill. In small bowl, combine all ingredients except chicken; mix until smooth. Onto four 12- to 14-inch metal skewers, loosely thread chicken strips.

2 When grill is heated, place skewers on gas grill over medium heat or on charcoal grill 4 to 6 inches from medium coals. Brush chicken with peanut butter mixture. Cook covered 8 to 10 minutes or until chicken is no longer pink in center, turning and brushing once with peanut butter mixture.

Broiled Chicken Satay: Place chicken on broiler pan; broil 4 to 6 inches from heat using times above as a guide, turning and brushing once with peanut butter mixture.

1 SERVING

Calories 140 (Calories from Fat 35);
Total Fat 4g (Saturated Fat 1g);
Cholesterol 65mg; Sodium 160mg;
Total Carbohydrates 1g (Dietary Fiber 0g);
Sugars 1g; Protein 25g

% Daily Value: Vitamin A 2%;
Vitamin C 0%; Calcium 0%; Iron 4%

Exchanges: 3 1/2 Very Lean Meat, 1/2 Fat

Carbohydrate Choices: 0

QUICK FIX

This recipe is a streamlined version of traditional marinated, grilled satay that is served with a peanut sauce. For this quicker version, the chicken is not marinated but is basted with the tasty sauce instead.

Honey-Glazed Chicken Thighs

■ ■ ■ ■ Ready in 20 minutes

4 servings

1/4 cup honey
2 tablespoons soy sauce
2 garlic cloves, minced, or 1/4 teaspoon garlic powder
4 boneless skinless chicken thighs (about 1 lb.)
2 tablespoons olive or vegetable oil
1/4 teaspoon salt
1/4 teaspoon coarse ground black pepper

1. Heat gas or charcoal grill. In small bowl, combine honey, soy sauce and garlic; blend well with wire whisk. Set aside. Brush chicken thighs with oil; sprinkle with salt and pepper.

2. When grill is heated, place chicken on gas grill over medium heat or on charcoal grill 4 to 6 inches from medium coals. Cook covered 8 to 12 minutes or until juice is clear when center of thickest part is cut (180°F), turning once and brushing with honey mixture during last 2 minutes of cooking time.

Broiled Honey-Glazed Chicken Thighs: Place chicken on broiler pan; broil 4 to 6 inches from heat using times above as a guide, turning once and brushing with honey mixture during last 2 minutes of cooking time.

1 SERVING

Calories 190 (Calories from Fat 90); **Total Fat 10g (Saturated Fat 3g); Cholesterol 70mg; Sodium 220mg; Total Carbohydrates 5g (Dietary Fiber 0g); Sugars 4g; Protein 20g**

% Daily Value: **Vitamin A 0%; Vitamin C 0%; Calcium 0%; Iron 6%**

Exchanges: **3 Lean Meat, 1/2 Other Carbohydrate**

Carbohydrate Choices: **0**

QUICK FIX

Use long-handled tongs to protect your hands from the heat of the grill and limit the amount of juices released from the chicken.

Chicken-Apple Burgers

■ ■ ■ ■ **Ready in 25 minutes**

4 sandwiches

1 medium apple, finely chopped (1 cup)
4 medium green onions, finely chopped (1/4 cup)
1 1/4 teaspoons poultry seasoning
1/2 teaspoon salt
2 tablespoons apple juice or water
1 lb. ground chicken or turkey
4 teaspoons honey mustard
4 burger buns, split
4 leaves leaf lettuce

1 Heat gas or charcoal grill. In medium bowl, combine apple, onions, poultry seasoning, salt and apple juice; mix well. Add ground chicken; mix well. Shape mixture into 4 (1/2-inch-thick) patties.

2 When grill is heated, carefully oil grill rack. Place patties on gas grill over medium heat or on charcoal grill 4 to 6 inches from medium coals. Cook covered 14 to 20 minutes or until thermometer inserted in center of patty reads 165°F, turning patties once.

3 Spread honey mustard on bottom halves of buns. Top each with lettuce, chicken patty and top half of bun. If desired, serve with additional honey mustard.

Broiled Chicken-Apple Burgers: Place patties on oiled broiler pan; broil 4 to 6 inches from heat using times above as a guide, turning once.

1 SANDWICH

Calories 360 (Calories from Fat 125);
Total Fat 14g (Saturated Fat 4g);
Cholesterol 75mg; Sodium 640mg;
Total Carbohydrates 31g (Dietary
Fiber 2g); Sugars 13g; Protein 27g

% Daily Value: Vitamin A 8%;
Vitamin C 4%; Calcium 8%; Iron 16%

Exchanges: 1 1/2 Starch, 3 Medium-Fat
Meat, 1/2 Other Carbohydrate

Carbohydrate Choices: 2

 QUICK FIX Planning ahead? Make up the chicken patties early in the day, and stack between pieces of waxed paper. Store in the refrigerator until dinnertime, then grill as directed in the recipe.

Chicken-Apple Burgers

Brown Sugar Barbecued Salmon
Whole Green Beans
Five-Layer Salad
Breadsticks

4 servings

1 Heat the grill. Cook the salmon.

2 While salmon cooks, make the salad.

3 Cook a box of frozen whole green beans in the microwave.

4 Bake a tube of refrigerated breadsticks or serve purchased breadsticks.

Five-Layer Salad

1 package (5 oz.) mixed salad greens
1 medium cucumber, peeled, seeded and coarsely chopped
1/2 cup three-cheese ranch salad dressing
1/4 cup cooked real bacon pieces (from 2.5-oz. package)
1/2 cup finely shredded Cheddar and Monterey Jack cheese
  blend (2 oz.)

1 SERVING

Calories 225 (Calories from Fat 180);
Total Fat 20g (Saturated Fat 6g);
Cholesterol 25mg; Sodium 480mg;
Total Carbohydrates 4g (Dietary
Fiber 1g); Sugars 4g; Protein 7g

% Daily Value: Vitamin A 26%;
Vitamin C 6%; Calcium 12%; Iron 4%

Exchanges: 1 Vegetable, 1/2 High-Fat
Meat, 3 Fat

Carbohydrate Choices: 0

1 On large serving platter or in large bowl, layer all ingredients.

2 To serve, spoon from platter or toss.

QUICK FIX

Make this pretty layered salad in a clear glass bowl as a main dish for lunch or a light dinner. Layer 2 cups of cubed ham or cooked chicken or turkey over the salad greens. Use only 2 tablespoons bacon pieces and sprinkle them over the top of the salad.

Brown Sugar Barbecued Salmon

1 (1-lb.) salmon fillet
1 teaspoon vegetable oil
1 tablespoon packed brown sugar
2 teaspoons cider vinegar
2 teaspoons honey mustard
1/8 to 1/4 teaspoon hot pepper sauce
Chopped fresh chives, if desired

1. Heat gas or charcoal grill. Brush skin side of salmon with oil. In small bowl, combine all remaining ingredients except chives; mix well. Spread over top of salmon.

2. When grill is heated, place salmon, skin side down, on gas grill over medium heat or on charcoal grill 4 to 6 inches from medium coals. Cook covered 10 to 14 minutes or until fish flakes easily with fork. Sprinkle with chives.

Broiled Brown Sugar Barbecued Salmon: Place salmon skin side down on broiler pan; broil 4 to 6 inches from heat using times above as a guide.

1 SERVING

Calories 180 (Calories from Fat 65); Total Fat 7g (Saturated Fat 2g); Cholesterol 75mg; Sodium 80mg; Total Carbohydrates 5g (Dietary Fiber 0g); Sugars 5g; Protein 24g

% Daily Value: Vitamin A 2%; Vitamin C 0%; Calcium 2%; Iron 4%

Exchanges: 2 Lean Meat, 2 Fat

Carbohydrate Choices: 0

QUICK FIX

Oiling the skin on the salmon helps to keep it from sticking. However, if you would like to serve the salmon without the skin, it is easy to do. When the fish is cooked, simply slide a metal turner between the fish and the skin and lift the fish from the grill, leaving the skin behind. The skin can be removed from the grill later.

Grilled Eggplant Parmesan

■ ■ ■ ■ **Ready in 25 minutes**   *4 servings*

1 medium red onion, cut into 8 wedges
1 (1 to 1 1/4-lb.) eggplant, peeled if desired, cut crosswise
    into 8 slices
Cooking spray
1/4 teaspoon salt
1/8 teaspoon pepper
1 jar (14 oz.) meatless tomato pasta sauce (2 cups)
1 cup shredded mozzarella cheese (4 oz.)
1/4 cup grated Parmesan cheese

1 Heat gas or charcoal grill. Onto one 12- to 14-inch metal skewer, thread onion wedges.

2 When grill is heated, spray onion wedges and eggplant slices with cooking spray; sprinkle with salt and pepper. Place on gas grill over medium-high heat or on charcoal grill 4 to 6 inches from medium-high coals. Cook covered 8 to 10 minutes or until tender, turning once.

3 Meanwhile, spray disposable 12 1/4 × 8 1/4-inch foil pan with cooking spray. Spread 1/2 cup of the pasta sauce in sprayed pan.

4 Arrange grilled eggplant slices over sauce. Top with remaining pasta sauce, grilled onion, mozzarella cheese and Parmesan cheese. Place pan on grill; cover loosely with foil. Cook 3 to 5 minutes or until sauce is bubbly and cheese is melted.

1 SERVING

Calories 230 (Calories from Fat 100); Total Fat 11g (Saturated Fat 5g); Cholesterol 20mg; Sodium 810mg; Total Carbohydrates 19g (Dietary Fiber 5g); Sugars 5g; Protein 13g

% Daily Value: Vitamin A 15%; Vitamin C 15%; Calcium 35%; Iron 6%

Exchanges: 1 Starch, 1 Vegetable, 1 Medium-Fat Meat, 1 Fat

Carbohydrate Choices: 1

QUICK FIX Don't have a disposable pan on hand? There's no need to make a special trip to get one; a 13 × 9-inch metal baking pan can be used in place of the disposable foil pan. To keep the pan from darkening, wrap the outside with foil.

Grilled Eggplant Parmesan

Five

Super Soups and Chowders

Superfast Ready in 15 minutes or less

Pasta Cheeseburger Soup

■ ■ ■ ■ Ready in 25 minutes

4 servings (1 1/2 cups each)

1 1/2 cups uncooked rotini pasta (4 oz.)
1/2 lb. lean (at least 80%) ground beef
2 small zucchini, chopped (2 cups)
1/2 teaspoon dried oregano leaves
1 tablespoon all-purpose flour
1/4 teaspoon salt
1 cup milk
1 cup chicken broth
1 jar (8 oz.) pasteurized process cheese sauce

1 Cook rotini as directed on package. Drain well.

2 Meanwhile, in 2 1/2-quart saucepan, cook ground beef, zucchini and oregano over medium-high heat for 5 to 7 minutes or until thoroughly cooked, stirring frequently. Drain.

3 Stir in flour and salt. Add milk, chicken broth, cheese sauce and cooked rotini to ground beef mixture; mix gently. Simmer about 5 minutes or until cheese is melted, stirring occasionally.

1 SERVING

Calories 430 (Calories from Fat 200); Total Fat 22g (Saturated Fat 11g); Cholesterol 80mg; Sodium 1,500mg; Total Carbohydrates 34g (Dietary Fiber 2g); Sugars 8g; Protein 25g

% Daily Value: Vitamin A 20%; Vitamin C 6%; Calcium 30%; Iron 15%

Exchanges: 2 Starch, 2 1/2 Medium-Fat Meat, 1 1/2 Fat

Carbohydrate Choices: 2

QUICK FIX
If you don't have rotini on hand, use elbow or shell macaroni. For an adult twist, use a cup of beer instead of the chicken broth.

Crossword Puzzle Soup
Peanut Butter and Banana Sandwiches
Caramelized Apple Sundaes

4 servings

1 Make the soup.

2 While the soup cooks, make the apples for the sundaes; remove from heat and let stand at room temperature.

3 For each sandwich, spread a slice of whole wheat bread with peanut butter; top with thin banana slices. Place another slice of bread on top; cut into quarters.

4 For dessert, spoon apple mixture over frozen yogurt.

Caramelized Apple Sundaes

2 medium Granny Smith apples
2 tablespoons butter or margarine
1/2 cup packed brown sugar
1/4 cup sweetened dried cranberries, if desired
1/8 teaspoon ground cinnamon
1/4 cup apple juice
1 pint (2 cups) frozen vanilla yogurt or ice cream

1 Peel and core apples. Cut into thin slices; cut each slice in half crosswise. In medium skillet, melt butter over medium heat. Add apples; cook 2 minutes, stirring frequently.

2 Add brown sugar, cranberries, cinnamon and apple juice; cook 6 to 8 minutes or until apples are tender and sauce is desired consistency, stirring occasionally.

3 To serve, spoon frozen yogurt into individual dessert dishes. Spoon apple mixture over frozen yogurt.

1 SERVING

Calories 300 (Calories from Fat 60); Total Fat 7g (Saturated Fat 4g); Cholesterol 20mg; Sodium 105mg; Total Carbohydrates 57g (Dietary Fiber 2g); Sugars 51g; Protein 4g

% Daily Value: Vitamin A 6%; Vitamin C 6%; Calcium 20%; Iron 4%

Exchanges: 1 Starch, 1 Fat, 3 Other Carbohydrates

Carbohydrate Choices: 4

QUICK FIX

The caramel-apple sauce can be made ahead and reheated in the microwave at serving time.

Crossword Puzzle Soup

1/2 lb. Italian sausage links, cut into 1/2-inch slices
2 cans (19 oz.) ready-to-serve tomato basil soup
1 cup frozen cut green beans (from 1-lb. bag)
3/4 cup uncooked alphabet macaroni
   (4 oz.)
1/4 cup shredded Parmesan cheese
   (1 oz.)

1. In 2-quart saucepan, cook sausage over medium heat until thoroughly cooked and no longer pink, stirring frequently. Drain.
2. Add soup and beans; mix well. Bring to a boil. Add macaroni; cook 5 to 10 minutes or until macaroni and beans are tender, stirring occasionally. Sprinkle individual servings with cheese.

QUICK FIX

Leftover soup is perfect to pack for lunches. Just heat individual servings in the microwave, and pour into a soup thermal container for lunch later.

1 SERVING

Calories 380 (Calories from Fat 140);
Total Fat 15g (Saturated Fat 5g);
Cholesterol 35mg; Sodium 1,350mg;
Total Carbohydrates 44g (Dietary
Fiber 2g); Sugars 13g; Protein 17g

% Daily Value: Vitamin A 15%;
Vitamin C 20%; Calcium 10%; Iron 15%

Exchanges: 2 Starch, 1 1/2 High-Fat Meat,
1/2 Fat, 1 Other Carbohydrate

Carbohydrate Choices: 3

Shrimp-Vegetable Noodle Soup

Ready in 25 minutes

4 servings (1 1/2 cups each)

2 cans (14 oz.) chicken broth
1 cup water
2 medium carrots, diagonally sliced (1 cup)
1 medium stalk celery, diagonally sliced (1/2 cup)
1 package (3 oz.) shrimp- or chicken-flavor ramen noodle soup
    mix, noodles partially broken
1 1/2 teaspoons grated gingerroot or 1/2 teaspoon
    ground ginger
1 teaspoon finely shredded lemon peel
1/8 teaspoon pepper
4 oz. (1 cup) fresh snow pea pods, cut in half diagonally
12 oz. uncooked peeled deveined medium shrimp, tails removed

1. In 3-quart saucepan, combine broth, water, carrots, celery, contents of seasoning packet from soup mix, gingerroot, lemon peel and pepper. Bring to a boil over medium-high heat. Cook 1 minute.

2. Add broken ramen noodles and pea pods; mix well. Reduce heat; simmer 2 minutes.

3. Stir in shrimp. Cook 3 to 4 minutes or until shrimp are pink and firm and soup is thoroughly heated, stirring occasionally.

1 SERVING

Calories 220 (Calories from Fat 50);
Total Fat 6g (Saturated Fat 3g);
Cholesterol 120mg; Sodium 1,150mg;
Total Carbohydrates 21g (Dietary
Fiber 2g); Sugars 4g; Protein 20g

% Daily Value: Vitamin A 210%;
Vitamin C 25%; Calcium 6%; Iron 20%

Exchanges: 1 1/2 Starch, 2 Very Lean Meat,
1/2 Fat

Carbohydrate Choices: 1 1/2

QUICK FIX

Make this soup even quicker by using cooked shrimp, adding them right at the end of the cooking time. They need to cook only 1 to 2 minutes, just long enough to heat them.

*Shrimp-Vegetable
Noodle Soup*

Asian Chicken Noodle Soup

■ ■ ■ ■ **Ready in 20 minutes**

4 servings (1 1/3 cups each)

4 cups water
2 medium green onions, sliced
1 teaspoon finely chopped gingerroot
1 package (3 oz.) oriental-flavor ramen noodle soup mix
2 medium stalks bok choy, sliced into 1/4-inch-thick slices (1 cup)
2 cups cooked chicken strips (about 1/4 inch wide)

1️⃣ In 2 1/2- to 3-quart saucepan, bring water, onions and gingerroot just to a boil over medium heat.

2️⃣ Increase heat to medium-high. Add ramen noodles; boil 2 minutes.

3️⃣ Add contents of seasoning packet from soup mix; stir to blend. Add bok choy; cook an additional 2 minutes. Stir in chicken strips; cook until thoroughly heated.

1 SERVING

Calories 220 (Calories from Fat 60);
Total Fat 7g (Saturated Fat 3g);
Cholesterol 60mg; Sodium 510mg;
Total Carbohydrates 14g (Dietary
Fiber 1g); Sugars 1g; Protein 24g

% Daily Value: Vitamin A 10%;
Vitamin C 10%; Calcium 4%; Iron 10%

Exchanges: 1 Starch, 3 Very Lean Meat,
1 Fat

Carbohydrate Choices: 1

QUICK FIX

No gingerroot on hand? Just use about 1/4 teaspoon ground ginger instead. If bok choy isn't a family favorite, use 1/2 cup thinly sliced celery and add it with the onions.

Southwestern Chicken Rice Soup

■ ■ ■ ■ Ready in 25 minutes

3 servings (1 1/2 cups each)

2 flour tortillas (8 inch)
1 cup cubed cooked chicken
6 medium green onions, chopped (1/3 cup)
1 can (19 oz.) ready-to-serve tomato basil soup
1 can (14 oz.) chicken broth
3/4 cup uncooked instant rice
1 teaspoon chopped fresh cilantro
2 teaspoons lime juice

1 Heat oven to 400°F. Cut tortillas into 1/4-inch strips; cut strips into 2- to 3-inch lengths. Place strips on ungreased cookie sheet. Bake for 6 to 8 minutes or until brown.

2 Meanwhile, in 1 1/2-quart saucepan, combine chicken, onions, soup and broth; mix well. Bring to a boil. Stir in rice. Remove from heat. Cover; let stand 5 minutes.

3 Stir cilantro and lime juice into soup. If necessary, simmer 5 minutes to heat thoroughly, stirring occasionally. Top individual servings with tortilla strips.

1 SERVING

Calories 340 (Calories from Fat 60); Total Fat 7g (Saturated Fat 2g); Cholesterol 40mg; Sodium 1,160mg; Total Carbohydrates 48g (Dietary Fiber 2g); Sugars 8g; Protein 22g

% Daily Value: Vitamin A 8%; Vitamin C 15%; Calcium 6%; Iron 20%

Exchanges: 2 1/2 Starch, 2 Lean Meat, 1/2 Other Carbohydrate

Carbohydrate Choices: 3

QUICK FIX

The crispy strips of flour tortilla that top this soup are delicious, but if you're in a hurry or don't want to heat the oven, you could top each serving with a few corn chips or broken tortilla chips instead.

Cheesy Pizza Soup *Superfast*

4 servings (1 1/4 cups each)

2 cans (19 oz.) ready-to-serve tomato basil soup
1/2 cup chopped pepperoni
1 1/2 cups shredded pizza cheese blend (6 oz.)
2 teaspoons chopped fresh basil or parsley, if desired

1. In 2-quart saucepan, combine soup, pepperoni and 1 cup of the cheese; mix well.

2. Cook over medium heat for 4 to 6 minutes or until thoroughly heated and cheese softens, stirring occasionally. (Cheese will not melt completely.) Top individual servings with remaining cheese and basil.

1 SERVING

Calories 400 (Calories from Fat 190); Total Fat 21g (Saturated Fat 10g); Cholesterol 40mg; Sodium 1,840mg; Total Carbohydrates 33g (Dietary Fiber 2g); Sugars 18g; Protein 17g

% Daily Value: Vitamin A 30%; Vitamin C 15%; Calcium 30%; Iron 8%

Exchanges: 1 1/2 Starch, 1 1/2 Other Carbs, 1 1/2 High-Fat Meat

Carbohydrate Choices: 3

QUICK FIX

For a flavor change, use 8 strips of cooked bacon, coarsely crumbled, instead of the pepperoni. You can find fully cooked bacon in the packaged meat department.

Sure, plastic food-storage bags work wonders for lunch bags and leftovers, but they also offer a wide array of unconventional uses.

1. Dump meat loaf or meatball ingredients in a large plastic food-storage bag. Press the air out, and seal the bag. Use your hands to squish the ingredients together and squeeze the mixture into a meat loaf pan. No messy hands or bowl to wash.

2. Turn a sandwich bag inside out and use it as a "glove" the next time you grease a pan. When you're finished, turn the bag right side out, seal it and store any leftover butter or shortening in the freezer.

3. Plastic food-storage bags are great stand-ins for pastry bags. Simply fill the bag with the ingredients of your choice, and snip off a small corner. Stuffing manicotti, filling mini muffin tins and frosting cookies has never been easier.

4. Put ground meat in a large resealable freezer bag. Flatten the bag, and store it in the freezer. The slab-like shape makes thawing a snap.

5. Freeze water in plastic food-storage bags, and use the frozen ice packs to keep food and beverages cold for barbecues, potlucks or picnics.

Goofy Face–Topped Soup

5 servings (3/4 cup each)

1 can (10.2 oz.) large refrigerated buttermilk homestyle
    biscuits (5 biscuits)
2 cans (18.5 or 19 oz.) any flavor ready-to-serve soup

1 SERVING

Calories 280 (Calories from Fat 90);
Total Fat 10g (Saturated Fat 2g);
Cholesterol 0mg; Sodium 1,560mg;
Total Carbohydrates 43g (Dietary
Fiber 1g); Sugars 14g; Protein 5g

% Daily Value: Vitamin A 6%;
Vitamin C 12%; Calcium 2%; Iron 12%

Exchanges: 1 1/2 Starch, 2 Fat, 1 1/2 Other
Carbohydrates

Carbohydrate Choices: 3

1   Heat oven to 350°F. Separate dough into 5 biscuits; place on ungreased cookie sheet. Press or roll each biscuit into 5-inch round.

2   Cut 6 (1/2-inch) slits on edge of one side of each biscuit to resemble hair. With small round cookie cutter, cut holes for mouth and eyes. Remove pieces from holes. Cut mouth cutouts in half; place on sides of biscuits for ears.

3   Bake for 13 to 17 minutes or until golden brown.

4   Meanwhile, heat soup in 2-quart saucepan as directed on can. Spoon soup into individual wide shallow bowls. Top each serving with biscuit head.

QUICK FIX

If you have frozen buttermilk biscuits on hand, go ahead and use them instead of the refrigerated type. Just let thaw at room temperature 5 minutes before shaping faces and follow the directions on the package for baking.

Tortellini and Bean Soup *Superfast*

▨ ▧ ▨ ▨ Ready in 15 minutes *4 servings (1 3/4 cups each)*

3 1/2 cups water
2 vegetable or chicken bouillon cubes
1 can (14.5 oz.) diced tomatoes with basil, garlic and oregano, undrained
1 cup frozen cut leaf spinach (from 1-lb. bag)
1 can (15 to 15.5 oz.) kidney beans, drained, rinsed
1 package (9 oz.) refrigerated cheese-filled tortellini

1 In 3-quart saucepan, combine water, bouillon and tomatoes. Bring to a boil over medium-high heat.

2 Add spinach, beans and tortellini; return to a boil. Reduce heat; boil gently 5 minutes or until tortellini is tender and soup is thoroughly heated, stirring occasionally.

1 SERVING

Calories 320 (Calories from Fat 45);
Total Fat 5g (Saturated Fat 2g);
Cholesterol 35mg; Sodium 1,170mg;
Total Carbohydrates 53g (Dietary
Fiber 7g); Sugars 5g; Protein 15g

% Daily Value: Vitamin A 30%;
Vitamin C 20%; Calcium 20%; Iron 20%

Exchanges: 3 Starch, 1 Vegetable, 1/2 Very
Lean Meat, 1/2 Fat

Carbohydrate Choices: 3

QUICK FIX

For a larger group or to have meals on hand for family members on the go, double the recipe and use a large saucepan to cook the soup. Servings can be quickly reheated in the microwave.

Corn and Bean Chili

5 servings (1 1/2 cups each)

1 lb. lean (at least 80%) ground beef
2 cans (15 oz.) spicy chili beans, undrained
1 can (14.5 oz.) diced tomatoes, undrained
1 can (11 oz.) vacuum-packed whole kernel corn, undrained
1 can (4.5 oz.) chopped green chiles

1. In 3-quart saucepan, cook ground beef over medium-high heat for 5 to 7 minutes or until thoroughly cooked, stirring frequently. Drain well; return to saucepan.

2. Add all remaining ingredients; mix well. Cook over medium heat for 10 to 15 minutes or until thoroughly heated and flavors are blended, stirring occasionally.

1 SERVING
Calories 420 (Calories from Fat 130);
Total Fat 14g (Saturated Fat 5g);
Cholesterol 55mg; Sodium 1,230mg;
Total Carbohydrates 47g (Dietary
Fiber 10g); Sugars 8g; Protein 26g

% Daily Value: Vitamin A 15%;
Vitamin C 20%; Calcium 10%; Iron 30%

Exchanges: 3 Starch, 2 Medium-Fat Meat

Carbohydrate Choices: 2 1/2

QUICK FIX

For super-easy cleanup, serve this tasty chili in sturdy disposable bowls. Sprinkle each serving with shredded Cheddar cheese, and add warm rolled tortillas to complete the meal.

Corn and Bean Chili

Chicken–Three Bean Chili
Honeydew Melon–Orange Salad
Tortilla Chips
Chocolate Pudding

4 servings

1 Make a box of chocolate pudding. Spoon into individual dishes; press plastic wrap on the surface and refrigerate.

2 Make the chili.

3 While the chili cooks, make the salad.

4 For dessert, top the pudding with whipped topping and sprinkle with mini chocolate chips.

Honeydew Melon–Orange Salad

1 tablespoon lime juice
1 tablespoon honey
1/4 teaspoon grated lime peel, if desired
3 cups cubed honeydew melon
1 can (11 oz.) mandarin orange segments, well drained

1 In medium bowl, combine lime juice, honey and lime peel; mix well.

2 Add melon and oranges; toss lightly. Serve immediately, or refrigerate until serving time.

1 SERVING
Calories 110 (Calories from Fat 0);
Total Fat 0g (Saturated Fat 0g);
Cholesterol 0mg; Sodium 20mg;
Total Carbohydrates 28g (Dietary
Fiber 1g); Sugars 23g; Protein 1g
% Daily Value: Vitamin A 8%;
Vitamin C 80%; Calcium 0%; Iron 2%
Exchanges: 2 Fruit
Carbohydrate Choices: 2

QUICK FIX

Buy cut-up honeydew melon in the refrigerator section of the supermarket to save time. If cut-up honeydew isn't available, use cut-up cantaloupe or fresh pineapple.

Chicken—Three Bean Chili

1 1/2 cups cubed cooked chicken

1 can (15 or 15.5 oz.) kidney beans, drained, rinsed

1 can (15 oz.) garbanzo beans, drained, rinsed

1 can (15 oz.) spicy chili beans, undrained

1 can (14.5 oz.) diced Mexican-style tomatoes, undrained

4 tablespoons sour cream, if desired

4 tablespoons green salsa, if desired

1. In 2 1/2- to 3-quart saucepan, combine all ingredients except sour cream and salsa.

2. Cook over medium heat for about 10 minutes or until thoroughly heated, stirring occasionally. Top individual servings with sour cream and salsa.

QUICK FIX

For speedy meals like this chili, keep cubed cooked chicken breast in the freezer. In a pinch, purchase roasted or baked chicken from the grocery store deli or the packaged meats department.

1 SERVING

Calories 565 (Calories from Fat 90); Total Fat 10g (Saturated Fat 3g); Cholesterol 55mg; Sodium 1,580mg; Total Carbohydrates 79g (Dietary Fiber 20g); Sugars 11g; Protein 40g

% Daily Value: Vitamin A 16%; Vitamin C 22%; Calcium 16%; Iron 52%

Exchanges: 5 Starch, 1 Vegetable, 3 1/2 Very Lean Meat, 1 1/2 Fat

Carbohydrate Choices: 4

Corny Potato Chowder *Superfast*

■ ■ ■ ■ **Ready in 15 minutes**

3 servings (1 cup each)

1 box (10 oz.) frozen cream-style corn in a pouch
1 can (18.5 oz.) ready-to-serve potato with ham and
    cheese chowder
3 tablespoons shredded Cheddar cheese
1 teaspoon chopped fresh parsley, if desired

1 Cook corn as directed on package.

2 Meanwhile, in 1 1/2-quart saucepan, cook soup over medium
heat for 4 to 5 minutes or until thoroughly heated, stirring
occasionally.

3 Remove cooked corn from pouch; add to soup. Cook 1 to 2
minutes or until mixture is thoroughly heated. Sprinkle
individual servings with cheese and parsley.

1 SERVING

Calories 240 (Calories from Fat 70);
Total Fat 8g (Saturated Fat 3g);
Cholesterol 15mg; Sodium 920mg;
Total Carbohydrates 34g (Dietary
Fiber 3g); Sugars 7g; Protein 8g

% Daily Value: Vitamin A 4%;
Vitamin C 6%; Calcium 10%; Iron 4%

Exchanges: 1 1/2 Starch, 1/2 Medium-Fat
Meat, 1 Fat, 1/2 Other Carbohydrate

Carbohydrate Choices: 2

QUICK FIX

This recipe will be even quicker if you substitute a can of cream-style corn for the frozen
type. You can omit the first step and just add the corn as directed in step 3.

Chipotle-Corn Chowder

■ ■ ■ **Ready in 25 minutes**

3 servings (1 2/3 cups each)

1 can (14.75 oz.) cream-style corn
1 can (11 oz.) vacuum-packed whole kernel corn with red and green peppers
1 teaspoon finely chopped chipotle chile in adobo sauce (from 11-oz. can)
1/4 teaspoon adobo sauce (from can of chipotle chiles)
1/8 teaspoon cumin
2 1/4 cups milk
2 tablespoons all-purpose flour
1/4 teaspoon salt

1 In 2-quart saucepan, combine cream-style corn, corn with peppers, chile, adobo sauce and cumin; mix well. Bring to a boil over medium-high heat, stirring frequently. Reduce heat; simmer 5 minutes to blend flavors, stirring frequently.

2 Meanwhile, in small bowl, combine 1/4 cup of the milk, flour and salt; beat with wire whisk until smooth.

3 Add remaining 2 cups milk to chowder. Stir in flour mixture until well blended. Cook over medium heat until bubbly and thickened, stirring constantly. Boil 1 minute.

1 SERVING

Calories 320 (Calories from Fat 45); Total Fat 5g (Saturated Fat 2g); Cholesterol 15mg; Sodium 1,340mg; Total Carbohydrates 57g (Dietary Fiber 4g); Sugars 27g; Protein 11g

% Daily Value: Vitamin A 15%; Vitamin C 8%; Calcium 25%; Iron 6%

Exchanges: 2 Starch, 1/2 Very Lean Meat, 1/2 Fat, 2 Other Carbohydrates

Carbohydrate Choices: 4

QUICK FIX

Make quick work of blending the milk and flour mixture in this and other recipes. Invest in a small jar with a tight-fitting lid. When it's time to mix this common thickening mixture, just measure, cover tightly and shake until blended!

Cheesy Hot Dog Chowder *Superfast*

■ ■ ■ ■ **Ready in 15 minutes**

4 servings (1 3/4 cups each)

2 cans (18.5 oz.) ready-to-serve 99% fat-free white Cheddar
    and potato soup
1 cup milk
1 cup frozen whole kernel corn (from 1-lb. bag)
4 hot dogs, thinly sliced
1 cup shredded American and Cheddar cheese blend (4 oz.)
Shredded American and Cheddar cheese blend, if desired

1. In 3-quart saucepan, combine soup, milk, corn and hot dogs;
   mix well. Bring to a boil. Reduce heat to medium-low; simmer
   6 to 8 minutes or until corn is tender, stirring occasionally.
2. Add 1 cup cheese; stir until melted. Top individual servings
   with additional shredded cheese.

1 SERVING

Calories 315 (Calories from Fat 205);
Total Fat 23g (Saturated Fat 11g);
Cholesterol 60mg; Sodium 850mg;
Total Carbohydrates 13g (Dietary
Fiber 1g); Sugars 6g; Protein 15g

% Daily Value: Vitamin A 10%;
Vitamin C 0%; Calcium 22%; Iron 4%

Exchanges: 1 Starch, 2 High-Fat Meat, 1 Fat

Carbohydrate Choices: 1

QUICK FIX

Looking for great food for youngsters? The ingredients for this kid-pleasing recipe are easy
to keep on hand so you can simmer up a yummy soup at a moment's notice.

Cheesy Hot Dog Chowder

Ham and Asparagus Chowder

■ ■ ■ ■ Ready in 20 minutes

4 servings (1 1/3 cups each)

2 medium unpeeled red potatoes, cubed (1 1/2 cups)
1/2 cup water
1 1/2 cups cut (1 1/2-inch) fresh asparagus spears
1 1/2 cups cubed cooked ham
1 can (10.75 oz.) condensed cream of mushroom soup
1 cup milk
Freshly ground black pepper, if desired

1. In 2-quart saucepan, bring potatoes and water to a boil. Reduce heat to medium; cover and cook 5 minutes or until potatoes are crisp-tender.
2. Add asparagus and ham; cover and cook 3 to 5 minutes or until thoroughly heated. Stir in soup and milk. Bring to a boil over high heat, stirring occasionally. Sprinkle individual servings with pepper.

1 SERVING

Calories 230 (Calories from Fat 70);
Total Fat 8g (Saturated Fat 3g);
Cholesterol 25mg; Sodium 990mg;
Total Carbohydrates 26g (Dietary
Fiber 2g); Sugars 8g; Protein 13g

% Daily Value: Vitamin A 10%;
Vitamin C 14%; Calcium 12%; Iron 10%

Exchanges: 2 Starch, 1 Lean Meat, 1 Fat

Carbohydrate Choices: 2

QUICK FIX

Frozen asparagus is a good substitute for the fresh in this recipe. You can use a 9-ounce package of asparagus cuts or 1 1/2 cups from a larger bag.

Ham and Asparagus Chowder

Coconut-Fish Chowder

■ ■ ■ ■ Ready in 25 minutes

4 servings (1 1/2 cups each)

1 cup uncooked instant rice
8 medium green onions, thinly sliced (1/2 cup)
1 medium red bell pepper, coarsely chopped (1 cup)
1 garlic clove, minced, or 1/8 teaspoon garlic powder
1 can (14 oz.) chicken broth
1 can (14 oz.) reduced-fat (lite) coconut milk (not cream of coconut)
1 tablespoon lime juice
1/2 teaspoon salt
1/8 teaspoon ground red pepper (cayenne)
1/8 teaspoon turmeric
1 lb. orange roughy fillets, cut into 1-inch pieces
1/4 cup chopped fresh cilantro
Sliced green onions, if desired

1 In 3-quart saucepan, combine all ingredients except fish, cilantro and sliced green onions. Bring to a boil.

2 Add fish. Reduce heat; simmer 5 to 8 minutes or until fish flakes easily with fork, stirring occasionally. Stir in cilantro. Sprinkle individual servings with sliced green onions.

1 SERVING

Calories 260 (Calories from Fat 60);
**Total Fat 7g (Saturated Fat 5g);
Cholesterol 25mg; Sodium 710mg;
Total Carbohydrates 26g (Dietary
Fiber 1g); Sugars 5g; Protein 22g**

% Daily Value: **Vitamin A 25%;
Vitamin C 45%; Calcium 8%; Iron 30%**

Exchanges: **1 1/2 Starch, 2 1/2 Very Lean
Meat, 1 Fat**

Carbohydrate Choices: **2**

QUICK FIX

Found in New Zealand's waters, orange roughy is a firm, white mild-flavored fish that's low in fat. Other firm white fish, such as cod, haddock or halibut, can be used in this chowder.

Quick Crab Bisque Superfast

■ ■ ■ ■ Ready in 15 minutes

4 servings (1 1/2 cups each)

1/4 cup butter or margarine
8 medium green onions, sliced (1/2 cup)
2 tablespoons all-purpose flour
1 teaspoon celery salt
1/8 teaspoon white pepper
1 quart (4 cups) milk
1 package (6 oz.) frozen crabmeat, thawed
1 cup whipping cream
1/4 cup dry sherry, if desired
Sliced green onion, if desired

1 In 3-quart saucepan, melt butter over medium heat. Add 1/2 cup sliced green onions; cook and stir until tender. Stir in flour, celery salt and pepper; cook 2 minutes, stirring occasionally.

2 Gradually add milk, cooking and stirring constantly over medium heat until mixture is slightly thickened. Stir in crabmeat, cream and sherry; cook just until thoroughly heated, stirring frequently. Sprinkle individual servings with green onions.

1 SERVING

Calories 410 (Calories from Fat 250);
Total Fat 28g (Saturated Fat 17g);
Cholesterol 115mg; Sodium 1,150mg;
Total Carbohydrates 18g (Dietary
Fiber 1g); Sugars 14g; Protein 18g

% Daily Value: Vitamin A 30%;
Vitamin C 10%; Calcium 35%; Iron 6%

Exchanges: 1 Starch, 2 Very Lean Meat,
5 Fat, 1/2 Other Carbohydrate

Carbohydrate Choices: 1

QUICK FIX

Don't have the frozen crabmeat on hand? Just substitute a can of crabmeat, drained and flaked, instead.

Speedy Main-Dish Salads

Superfast Ready in 15 minutes or less

Pepper Steak Salad

■ ■ ■ ■ **Ready in 20 minutes**

4 servings (1 1/3 cups each)

Dressing
1/4 cup vegetable oil
3 tablespoons red wine vinegar
2 tablespoons Dijon mustard
1 tablespoon soy sauce
1/4 teaspoon pepper
1 garlic clove, minced, or 1/8 teaspoon garlic powder

Salad
2 1/2 cups shredded Chinese (napa) cabbage
1/2 lb. cooked roast beef, cut into strips or chunks
    (about 1 1/3 cups)
1 cup cherry tomatoes, halved
1 cup sliced fresh mushrooms
2 medium stalks celery, sliced (1/2 cup)
1/2 large green bell pepper, cut into bite-size strips

1 In large bowl, combine dressing ingredients; blend well.
2 Add all salad ingredients; toss gently to coat. Serve
   immediately.

1 SERVING

Calories 230 (Calories from Fat 140);
Total Fat 16g (Saturated Fat 2g);
Cholesterol 25mg; Sodium 1,070mg;
Total Carbohydrates 7g (Dietary Fiber 2g);
Sugars 2g; Protein 14g

% Daily Value: Vitamin A 30%;
Vitamin C 60%; Calcium 6%; Iron 15%

Exchanges: 1 Vegetable, 1 1/2 Medium-Fat
Meat, 2 Fat

Carbohydrate Choices: 1/2

QUICK FIX

The shredded Chinese cabbage is delicious in this recipe, but if you're short on time, pick
up a bag of finely shredded cabbage in the produce department to use instead.

Ham and Vegetable Pasta Salad
Chili Cheese Bread
Oranges with Honey and Walnuts

4 servings

1 Make the pasta salad; cover and refrigerate.

2 Peel and slice 4 oranges; cover and refrigerate.

3 Heat the broiler. Broil the bread.

4 For dessert, arrange orange slices on individual plates. Drizzle with honey and sprinkle with chopped walnuts.

Chili Cheese Bread

1/4 cup light chives and onion cream cheese spread
  (from 8-oz. container)
2 tablespoons chopped green chiles (from 4.5-oz. can), drained
1/2 loaf French bread (16 inches long), halved lengthwise
1/2 cup reduced-fat shredded Cheddar and Monterey Jack
  cheese blend (2 oz.)

1 In small bowl, combine cream cheese and chiles.

2 Place bread halves, cut sides up, on broiler pan. Broil 4 to 6 inches from heat for 1 to 2 minutes or until light golden brown.

3 Top with cream cheese mixture and shredded cheese. Broil additional 2 minutes or until cheese is melted. Cut each bread half into 4 pieces.

1 SERVING
Calories 115 (Calories from Fat 35); Total Fat 4g (Saturated Fat 2g); Cholesterol 10mg; Sodium 270mg; Total Carbohydrates 15g (Dietary Fiber 0g); Sugars 1g; Protein 5g
% Daily Value: Vitamin A 4%; Vitamin C 0%; Calcium 8%; Iron 4%
Exchanges: 1 Starch, 1 Fat
Carbohydrate Choices: 1

QUICK FIX

For nacho-flavored cheese bread, add 1 1/2 teaspoons taco seasoning mix (from a 1.25-ounce package) with the cream cheese.

Ham and Vegetable Pasta Salad

Dressing
3/4 cup mayonnaise or salad dressing
1/4 cup milk
2 tablespoons chopped fresh or
    1 1/2 teaspoons dried dill
2 tablespoons Dijon mustard

Salad
2 cups uncooked small pasta shells (7 oz.)
1 cup diced cooked ham
1 small unpeeled cucumber, diced (1 cup)
1 small carrot, finely chopped (1/2 cup)
1/4 cup chopped red bell pepper
4 medium green onions, finely chopped
    (1/4 cup)

1. Cook pasta as directed on package. Drain; rinse with cold water to cool. Drain well.
2. Meanwhile, in large bowl, combine dressing ingredients; blend well.
3. Add cooked pasta and all remaining salad ingredients to dressing; toss to coat. Serve immediately, or cover and refrigerate until serving time.

1 SERVING
Calories 570 (Calories from Fat 330);
Total Fat 37g (Saturated Fat 6g);
Cholesterol 40mg; Sodium 950mg;
Total Carbohydrates 43g (Dietary
Fiber 2g); Sugars 6g; Protein 15g
% Daily Value: Vitamin A 100%;
Vitamin C 30%; Calcium 6%; Iron 15%
Exchanges: 2 1/2 Starch, 1 Vegetable,
1 Lean Meat, 6 1/2 Fat
Carbohydrate Choices: 3

QUICK FIX

Save on cleanup with disposable cutting sheets, available at grocery and discount stores. The sheets come in packages of about 20 and are perfect to use when you are in a hurry. Just chop, slice and dice your ingredients, then toss the sheet—and the mess—away!

Chips 'n Salsa Taco Salad

■ ■ ■ ■ **Ready in 20 minutes**

4 servings (2 cups each)

Salad

3/4 lb. coarse ground pork for chow mein
    or coarse ground beef for chili
1 medium onion, sliced, separated into rings
2 tablespoons taco seasoning mix
    (from 1.25-oz. package)
3/4 cup chunky-style salsa
4 cups shredded lettuce
2 cups broken tortilla chips
2 medium tomatoes, chopped
1 cup shredded Mexican cheese blend
    or Cheddar cheese (4 oz.)

Dressing

1/2 cup chunky-style salsa
1/4 cup French salad dressing

Garnishes

Sliced or cubed avocado
Sliced ripe olives
Sour cream
Chunky-style salsa
Whole tortilla chips

1. Spray 10-inch nonstick skillet with cooking spray. Add pork and onion; cook over medium heat 7 to 10 minutes or until no longer pink, stirring frequently.

2. Stir in taco seasoning mix and 3/4 cup salsa. Cook 2 to 3 minutes or until thoroughly heated and sauce is of desired consistency, stirring occasionally.

3. In large bowl, combine dressing ingredients; blend well. Add meat mixture, lettuce, broken chips and tomatoes; toss to mix. Spoon onto individual serving plates. Sprinkle salads with cheese. Garnish as desired.

1 SERVING

Calories 800 (Calories from Fat 460); Total Fat 51g (Saturated Fat 18g); Cholesterol 85mg; Sodium 2,220mg; Total Carbohydrates 56g (Dietary Fiber 10g); Sugars 14g; Protein 29g

% Daily Value: Vitamin A 60%; Vitamin C 40%; Calcium 35%; Iron 25%

Exchanges: 3 1/2 Starch, 1 Vegetable, 2 1/2 High-Fat Meat, 6 Fat, 1 Other Carbohydrate

Carbohydrate Choices: 3

QUICK FIX

Spatter does matter, so cut down on stovetop spatters by topping your skillet with a mesh spatter screen. Unlike a solid lid, the mesh screen allows steam to escape so food fries rather than steams. Look for this handy gadget in discount and department stores.

When it comes to avoiding sticky situations, cooking spray can't be beat. Even so, the following five uses may surprise you.

1. Spray your kitchen scissors with cooking spray the next time you need to cut up dried fruit or marshmallows.

2. Keep leftover avocado halves looking fresh by lightly spraying the exposed flesh with cooking spray. Wrap the avocado half in foil and refrigerate.

3. Spray the inside of a measuring cup with cooking spray to keep ingredients like honey and molasses from sticking to the measuring cup.

4. For fuss-free flipping, spray both sides of a spatula with cooking spray when making pancakes or egg dishes.

5. Spray colanders or strainers with cooking spray before draining pasta or potatoes.

Cooking Spray

Chicken and Cannellini Bean Salad

■ ■ ■ ■ **Ready in 20 minutes**

4 servings (1 1/4 cups each)

Vinaigrette
2 teaspoons finely chopped fresh rosemary
1/2 teaspoon salt
1/8 teaspoon pepper
3 tablespoons white balsamic vinegar
1 teaspoon Dijon mustard
1/4 cup extra-virgin olive oil

Salad
1 1/2 cups cubed cooked chicken
1/4 cup diced red onion
1 medium red bell pepper, cut into bite-size strips
1 small zucchini, halved lengthwise, sliced (1 cup)
1 can (15 oz.) cannellini beans, drained, rinsed

1. In medium bowl, combine rosemary, salt, pepper, vinegar mustard; mix well with wire whisk. Gradually beat in oil until well blended.
2. Add all salad ingredients; toss to coat. Serve immediately, or cover and refrigerate until serving time.

1 SERVING

Calories 305 (Calories from Fat 155);
Total Fat 17g (Saturated Fat 3g);
Cholesterol 45mg; Sodium 380mg;
Total Carbohydrates 31g (Dietary
Fiber 8g); Sugars 4g; Protein 25g

% Daily Value: Vitamin A 40%;
Vitamin C 100%; Calcium 12%; Iron 28%

Exchanges: 2 Starch, 3 Lean Meat

Carbohydrate Choices: 2

QUICK FIX

There's no need to cook chicken for recipes like this. Cooked chicken is readily available in the deli, in packages in the fresh meat counter and frozen. The frozen variety is great to have on hand for quick meals at a moment's notice.

Chicken Nugget Caesar Salad

■ ■ ■ Ready in 20 minutes

4 servings (1 3/4 cups each)

1 package (10 oz.) frozen breaded chicken breast chunks
4 cups torn romaine lettuce
1 cup halved cherry tomatoes
5 oz. mozzarella cheese, cut into small cubes (1 cup)
1/2 cup Caesar salad dressing

1 Cook chicken breast chunks as directed on package.

2 Meanwhile, in large bowl, combine lettuce, tomatoes and cheese. If desired, cut warm chicken chunks in half. Add chicken and salad dressing to salad; toss to coat. Serve immediately.

1 SERVING

Calories 410 (Calories from Fat 260);
Total Fat 29g (Saturated Fat 9g);
Cholesterol 55mg; Sodium 970mg;
Total Carbohydrates 15g (Dietary
Fiber 1g); Sugars 3g; Protein 22g

% Daily Value: Vitamin A 40%;
Vitamin C 20%; Calcium 30%; Iron 8%

Exchanges: 1/2 Starch, 1 Vegetable,
2 1/2 Medium-Fat Meat, 3 1/2 Fat

Carbohydrate Choices: 1

QUICK FIX

There's no need to spend time cutting cheese into cubes. For snacks or recipes like this easy salad, look for cubes of a variety of cheeses in small bags in the shredded cheese area of the grocery store.

Greek Chicken Salad

6 servings (2 1/2 cups each)

Dressing
3/4 cup Italian salad dressing
1 1/2 teaspoons dried dill weed

Salad
12 cups loosely packed torn romaine lettuce
1 purchased rotisserie chicken, meat removed from bone, thinly sliced
1 pint (2 cups) cherry tomatoes, halved
1 large cucumber, halved, seeded and sliced
3/4 cup pitted Kalamata olives
6 thin slices red onion, separated into rings
1 package (4 oz.) crumbled feta cheese

1. In large bowl, combine dressing ingredients; blend well.
2. Add lettuce, chicken, tomatoes, cucumber, olives and onion; toss to coat. Arrange salad on individual serving plates; sprinkle with cheese.

1 SERVING

Calories 400 (Calories from Fat 250);
Total Fat 28g (Saturated Fat 6g);
Cholesterol 80mg; Sodium 780mg;
Total Carbohydrates 12g (Dietary
Fiber 3g); Sugars 8g; Protein 26g

% Daily Value: Vitamin A 70%;
Vitamin C 60%; Calcium 15%; Iron 15%

Exchanges: 2 Vegetable, 3 Very Lean
Meat, 5 1/2 Fat

Carbohydrate Choices: 1

QUICK FIX

There's no need to wash and cut up romaine anymore! Just look for bags of ready-to-use romaine in the produce area. Or try any of the other bags of salad green blends in this salad.

Greek Chicken Salad

Ranch Club Salad *Superfast*

4 servings (1 1/2 cups each)

8 cups shredded lettuce
1 (3/4-lb.) chunk cooked turkey breast (from deli), cut
    into 2 × 1/4-inch strips
4 slices purchased cooked bacon, cut into 1/2-inch pieces
1 small tomato, chopped
1 cup seasoned croutons
1/2 cup ranch salad dressing

1 In large bowl, combine all ingredients except dressing.
2 Add dressing; toss to coat.

1 SERVING

Calories 340 (Calories from Fat 200);
Total Fat 22g (Saturated Fat 5g);
Cholesterol 70mg; Sodium 540mg;
Total Carbohydrates 12g (Dietary
Fiber 2g); Sugars 3g; Protein 24g

% Daily Value: Vitamin A 10%;
Vitamin C 15%; Calcium 6%; Iron 15%

Exchanges: 3 1/2 Lean Meat, 2 Fat, 1 Other
Carbohydrate

Carbohydrate Choices: 1

QUICK FIX

If you have the 10-ounce bags of salad greens on hand, use them instead of shredding head
lettuce. The lettuce in about 1 1/2 bags is equal to 8 cups of shredded greens.

Ranch Club Salad

Crunchy Asian Chicken Salad

■ ■ ■ ■ **Ready in 20 minutes**

4 servings (1 1/2 cups each)

Salad
1 tablespoon butter or margarine
1 package (3 oz.) oriental-flavor ramen noodle soup mix,
    noodles crushed
2 cups coleslaw blend (from 16-oz. bag)
2 cups shredded lettuce
1 package (9 oz.) frozen diced cooked chicken, thawed,
    larger pieces cut up if necessary
1/4 cup chopped peanuts
2 medium green onions, sliced (2 tablespoons)

Dressing
1/3 cup rice vinegar or white vinegar
1/4 cup creamy peanut butter
3 tablespoons sugar
2 tablespoons vegetable oil
Contents of seasoning packet from soup mix

1. In 8-inch skillet, melt butter over medium heat. Add crushed ramen noodles; cook 4 to 5 minutes or until toasted, stirring constantly.
2. Meanwhile, in large bowl, combine dressing ingredients; blend well.
3. Add toasted noodles, coleslaw blend, lettuce and chicken; toss to coat. If desired, serve on lettuce-lined plates. Sprinkle with peanuts and onions.

1 SERVING

Calories 420 (Calories from Fat 235);
Total Fat 26g (Saturated Fat 6g);
Cholesterol 60mg; Sodium 460mg;
Total Carbohydrates 20g (Dietary
Fiber 3g); Sugars 13g; Protein 27g

% Daily Value: Vitamin A 6%;
Vitamin C 22%; Calcium 4%; Iron 10%

Exchanges: 1 Starch, 1 Vegetable, 3 Very
Lean Meat, 4 1/2 Fat

Carbohydrate Choices: 1

QUICK FIX

Although the dressing for this salad is delicious, if you are pressed for time, go ahead and substitute about 3/4 cup purchased Asian salad dressing. You'll find a variety of brands to choose from.

Antipasto Salad
with Balsamic Vinaigrette

 **Ready in 20 minutes** *6 servings (1 1/2 cups each)*

Vinaigrette
1/4 cup balsamic vinegar
1/4 cup olive oil
2 tablespoons chopped fresh parsley
1 teaspoon sugar
1/2 teaspoon salt

Salad
4 cups shredded romaine lettuce
4 oz. sliced cooked chicken or turkey, cut into bite-size strips (1 cup)
4 oz. sliced salami or summer sausage, cut into bite-size strips
     (1 cup)
2 oz. sliced mozzarella cheese, cut into bite-size strips (1/2 cup)
2 cups fresh cauliflower florets
1 small cucumber, sliced (1 cup)
1 medium tomato, cut into thin wedges
1 yellow, red or green bell pepper, coarsely chopped (1 cup)

1 In small bowl, combine vinaigrette ingredients; blend well.
2 Arrange lettuce on individual serving plates. Arrange chicken, salami, cheese, cauliflower, cucumber and tomato over lettuce. Sprinkle with bell pepper. Drizzle vinaigrette over salads.

1 SERVING

Calories 220 (Calories from Fat 140);
Total Fat 16g (Saturated Fat 4g);
Cholesterol 35mg; Sodium 480mg;
Total Carbohydrates 8g (Dietary
Fiber 2g); Sugars 5g; Protein 12g

% Daily Value: Vitamin A 25%;
Vitamin C 130%; Calcium 10%; Iron 8%

Exchanges: 1 Vegetable, 1 1/2 Medium-Fat
Meat, 2 Fat

Carbohydrate Choices: 1/2

 QUICK FIX Shortcuts for this recipe include a stop in the produce area for a bag of shredded romaine and a package of precut cauliflower florets, then a quick stop at the salad bar for the rest of the vegetables. Pick up the chicken and sausage in the deli, and you're ready to go!

Cajun Chicken Salad

4 servings (1 1/2 cups each)

Dressing

2 tablespoons cider vinegar
2 to 3 teaspoons dried Cajun seasoning
1/3 cup vegetable oil

Salad

1 package (9 oz.) frozen diced cooked chicken breast, thawed
2 cups cold cooked rice
3 stalks celery, diced (1 cup)
6 medium green onions, chopped (1/3 cup)
1 large tomato, diced (1 cup)
1 medium green bell pepper, diced (1 cup)

1   In large bowl, combine vinegar and Cajun seasoning; mix well with wire whisk. Gradually beat in oil until well blended.

2   Add salad ingredients; toss to coat. Serve immediately, or cover and refrigerate until serving time.

1 SERVING

Calories 485 (Calories from Fat 200);
Total Fat 22g (Saturated Fat 4g);
Cholesterol 55mg; Sodium 300mg;
Total Carbohydrates 47g (Dietary
Fiber 2g); Sugars 3g; Protein 25g

% Daily Value: Vitamin A 16%;
Vitamin C 64%; Calcium 4%; Iron 16%

Exchanges: 3 Starch, 2 1/2 Very Lean
Meat, 4 Fat

Carbohydrate Choices: 3

QUICK FIX

With a little planning ahead you can have cooked rice in the refrigerator ready to go. When you are cooking rice, add an extra cup of uncooked rice to the pot so you have 2 cups of leftover rice. Or, stop at an Asian restaurant and buy 2 cups of cooked rice.

Cajun Chicken Salad

Shrimp and Mango Salad
Cheesy Tortillas
Orange-Pineapple Twister

4 servings

1 Make the shrimp mixture for the salad.

2 Heat 4 flour tortillas as directed on the package. Spread each with butter and sprinkle generously with shredded Parmesan cheese. Fold in half; cut into 3 wedges.

3 Spoon the shrimp mixture onto the salad greens and sprinkle with nuts.

4 Make the orange-pineapple beverage.

Orange-Pineapple Twister

2 cans (20 oz.) pineapple chunks
   in unsweetened juice, chilled, drained
1 pint (2 cups) orange sherbet
1/2 cup skim milk

1 In blender container or food processor bowl with metal blade, blend pineapple until smooth.

2 Spoon sherbet into container; add milk. Cover; blend until smooth. Serve immediately.

1 SERVING

Calories 300 (Calories from Fat 15);
Total Fat 2g (Saturated Fat 1g);
Cholesterol 5mg; Sodium 55mg;
Total Carbohydrates 68g (Dietary
Fiber 3g); Sugars 58g; Protein 3g

% Daily Value: Vitamin A 4%;
Vitamin C 50%; Calcium 10%; Iron 6%

Exchanges: 1 Starch, 2 Fruit, 1 1/2 Other
Carbohydrates

Carbohydrate Choices: 4 1/2

QUICK FIX

When fresh pineapple is at its peak, you may want to use 4 cups cubed fresh pineapple instead of the canned. And try other flavors of sherbet, such as lime, lemon or pineapple.

Shrimp and Mango Salad

Dressing
1/3 cup frozen concentrated limeade mix, thawed

2 tablespoons orange marmalade

2 tablespoons vegetable oil

Salad
1 lb. cooked peeled deveined medium shrimp, tails removed

1 1/2 cups cubed unpeeled seedless cucumber

1/2 medium red bell pepper, chopped (1/2 cup)

2 ripe medium mangoes, peeled, seeds removed and chopped

1 fresh jalapeño chile, seeded, finely chopped

4 cups mixed baby salad greens

1/4 cup chopped macadamia nuts or almonds, toasted, if desired

 In medium bowl, combine dressing ingredients; blend well. Add shrimp, cucumber, bell pepper, mangoes and chili; toss to coat.

2 Arrange salad greens on individual serving plates. Spoon shrimp mixture onto salad greens. Sprinkle with nuts.

1 SERVING
Calories 390 (Calories from Fat 140); Total Fat 15g (Saturated Fat 2g); Cholesterol 220mg; Sodium 270mg; Total Carbohydrates 38g (Dietary Fiber 4g); Sugars 30g; Protein 26g
% Daily Value: Vitamin A 110%; Vitamin C 120%; Calcium 10%; Iron 25%
Exchanges: 1 Fruit, 1 Vegetable, 3 1/2 Very Lean Meat, 2 1/2 Fat, 1 Other Carbohydrate
Carbohydrate Choices: 2 1/2

QUICK FIX
If fresh mangoes aren't available, you can use sliced mangoes from a jar found in the refrigerated produce area of the grocery store. Or use 2 large ripe fresh or 4 canned peach halves instead of mangoes.

Pesto Shrimp and Shells Salad

5 servings (1 1/2 cups each)

3 cups uncooked medium pasta shells (8 oz.)
1 box (9 oz.) frozen sugar snap peas in a pouch
1/3 cup refrigerated basil pesto (from 7-oz. container)
1/4 cup light mayonnaise or salad dressing
1 package (12 oz.) frozen cooked medium shrimp with tails
    removed, thawed, rinsed
1 medium tomato, chopped (3/4 cup)
2 medium green onions, chopped (2 tablespoons)
4 teaspoons shredded Parmesan cheese

1. Cook pasta as directed on package, adding frozen sugar snap peas during last 2 minutes of cooking time. Drain; rinse with cold water to cool. Drain well.

2. In large bowl, combine pesto and mayonnaise; mix well. Add cooked pasta, sugar snap peas, shrimp, tomato and onions; stir gently to mix. Sprinkle with cheese. If desired, serve salad on lettuce-lined plates.

1 SERVING

Calories 405 (Calories from Fat 135); Total Fat 15g (Saturated Fat 3g); Cholesterol 140mg; Sodium 580mg; Total Carbohydrates 43g (Dietary Fiber 3g); Sugars 5g; Protein 24g

% Daily Value: Vitamin A 14%; Vitamin C 24%; Calcium 14%; Iron 30%

Exchanges: 3 Starch, 2 Very Lean Meat, 3 Fat

Carbohydrate Choices: 3

QUICK FIX

Thaw the shrimp quickly by placing them in a colander and running cold water over them until they are thawed.

Tortellini-Tuna Salad

■ ■ ■ **Ready in 20 minutes**

4 servings (2 cups each)

1 package (9 oz.) refrigerated cheese-filled tortellini
1/2 cup fresh baby-cut carrots, cut into 1/2-inch chunks
1 can (6 oz.) albacore tuna in spring water, drained, flaked
1 medium stalk celery, sliced (1/2 cup)
1/2 cup light or regular three-cheese ranch salad dressing
4 cups mixed salad greens

1. Cook tortellini as directed on package, adding carrots during last 3 minutes of cooking time. Drain; rinse with cold water to cool. Drain well.
2. Meanwhile, in large bowl, combine all remaining ingredients except salad greens.
3. Add cooked tortellini and carrots to salad; mix well. Arrange salad greens on individual serving plates; spoon salad onto greens.

1 SERVING

Calories 240 (Calories from Fat 110); Total Fat 12g (Saturated Fat 3g); Cholesterol 65mg; Sodium 520mg; Total Carbohydrates 17g (Dietary Fiber 2g); Sugars 5g; Protein 17g

% Daily Value: Vitamin A 100%; Vitamin C 10%; Calcium 10%; Iron 15%

Exchanges: 1 Starch, 1 Vegetable, 1 1/2 Lean Meat, 1 1/2 Fat

Carbohydrate Choices: 1

QUICK FIX

Look for tuna that is packaged in sealed pouches instead of cans. There's no need for that pesky draining!

Crispy Fish–Asian Pasta Salad

4 servings (1 1/2 cups each)

Salad

2 1/2 cups uncooked farfalle (bow-tie) pasta (6 oz.)
1 cup frozen sugar snap peas (from 1-lb. bag)
12 frozen breaded fish sticks
2 cups coleslaw blend (from 16-oz. bag)
1/2 medium red bell pepper, chopped (1/2 cup)
4 cups torn iceberg and romaine lettuce blend (from 11-oz. bag)

Dressing

1/3 cup mayonnaise or salad dressing
1/3 cup Asian vinaigrette or vinegar and oil vinaigrette

1. Cook pasta as directed on package, adding sugar snap peas during last 3 minutes of cooking time. Drain; rinse with cold water to cool. Drain well.

2. Meanwhile, cook fish sticks as directed on package. Carefully cut each fish stick into 3 or 4 pieces.

3. In large bowl, combine dressing ingredients; mix well. Add cooked pasta and sugar snap peas, coleslaw blend and bell pepper; stir to coat. Add fish sticks; stir gently to mix. Arrange lettuce blend on individual serving plates. Spoon salad onto lettuce.

1 SERVING

Calories 510 (Calories from Fat 215); Total Fat 24g (Saturated Fat 4g); Cholesterol 25mg; Sodium 840mg; Total Carbohydrates 58g (Dietary Fiber 4g); Sugars 14g; Protein 15g

% Daily Value: Vitamin A 38%; Vitamin C 50%; Calcium 14%; Iron 20%

Exchanges: 3 1/2 Starch, 1 Vegetable, 1/2 Medium-Fat Meat, 4 Fat

Carbohydrate Choices: 4

QUICK FIX Try this salad with a 10-ounce package of frozen breaded chicken breast chunks. Just cook the chicken as directed on package.

Crispy Fish—Asian Pasta Salad

Italian Tortellini–Vegetable Salad
Crusty Whole Wheat Dinner Rolls
Pineapple Caramel Sundae

8 servings

1 Make the tortellini pasta salad; cover and refrigerate.

2 Heat the broiler. Broil the pineapple for the sundaes; let stand at room temperature.

3 Heat the oven. Heat the frozen whole wheat dinner rolls as directed on bag.

4 For dessert, top the pineapple with frozen yogurt, caramel sauce and nuts.

Pineapple Caramel Sundae

1 can (20 oz.) pineapple slices in unsweetened juice, drained
1/2 cup packed light brown sugar
1 quart (4 cups) vanilla frozen yogurt or ice cream
1/2 cup caramel ice cream topping
1 cup coarsely chopped toasted almonds, if desired

1 On ungreased cookie sheet, place pineapple slices. Sprinkle 1/4 cup of the brown sugar evenly over pineapple. Broil 3 inches from heat about 4 minutes or until lightly brown. Turn pineapple over; sprinkle with remaining 1/4 cup brown sugar. Broil an additional 4 minutes. Cool.

2 To serve, place pineapple on dessert plates or in bowls. Top each with scoop of frozen yogurt. Drizzle each with caramel topping; sprinkle with almonds.

1 SERVING

Calories 250 (Calories from Fat 10);
Total Fat 1g (Saturated Fat 1g);
Cholesterol 5mg; Sodium 135mg;
Total Carbohydrates 56g (Dietary Fiber 1g);
Sugars 50g; Protein 5g

% Daily Value: Vitamin A 2%;
Vitamin C 10%; Calcium 20%; Iron 4%

Exchanges: 1 Starch, 3 Other Carbohydrates

Carbohydrate Choices: 4

QUICK FIX Short on time? Place the pineapple slices on dessert plates and sprinkle with 1/4 cup brown sugar. Top with yogurt, caramel topping and almonds.

Italian Tortellini–Vegetable Salad

1 package (9 oz.) refrigerated
   cheese-filled tortellini
1 package (9 oz.) refrigerated
   spinach-filled tortellini
2 cups small fresh cauliflower
   florets
2 cups small fresh broccoli florets
1 cup oil-packed julienne-cut
   sun-dried tomatoes (from
   6.5-oz. jar), drained
1/4 cup chopped red onion
1/4 cup chopped fresh parsley
1 medium yellow bell pepper, chopped (1 cup)
2 jars (6 oz.) marinated artichoke hearts, drained,
   coarsely chopped and reserving 1/4 cup liquid
1 bottle (8 oz.) Italian salad dressing

1   In 4-quart saucepan or Dutch oven, cook tortellini as directed on package, adding cauliflower and broccoli during last minute of cooking time. Drain; rinse with cold water to cool. Drain well.

2   Meanwhile, in large bowl, combine tomatoes, onion, parsley, bell pepper and artichokes.

3   Add cooked tortellini, cauliflower and broccoli to salad; stir gently to mix. Add salad dressing and reserved 1/4 cup artichoke liquid; toss to coat. Serve immediately, or cover and refrigerate until serving time.

1 SERVING

Calories 355 (Calories from Fat 205);
Total Fat 23g (Saturated Fat 4g);
Cholesterol 75mg; Sodium 600mg; Total
Carbohydrates 27g (Dietary Fiber 4g);
Sugars 8g; Protein 10g

% Daily Value: Vitamin A 22%;
Vitamin C 64%; Calcium 14%; Iron 12%

Exchanges: 1 1/2 Starch, 1 Vegetable,
1/2 High-Fat Meat, 4 Fat

Carbohydrate Choices: 2

QUICK FIX   Save on prep time by using frozen broccoli and cauliflower florets. Both vegetables are available in bags for easy measuring. You'll need to add the frozen vegetables during the last 3 minutes of the tortellini cooking time.

Creamy Pasta-Bean Salad

4 servings (1 1/3 cups each)

Salad

1 1/2 cups uncooked rotini pasta

1 can (15 or 15.5 oz.) garbanzo beans, drained, rinsed

1 1/2 cups halved cherry tomatoes

1/2 medium green bell pepper, cut into 1/2-inch pieces

Dressing

1/2 cup light mayonnaise or salad dressing

1/4 cup shredded or grated Parmesan cheese (1 oz.)

1 tablespoon chopped fresh or 3/4 teaspoon dried basil

1 tablespoon cider vinegar

1/4 teaspoon salt

1 Cook rotini as directed on package. Drain; rinse with cold water to cool. Drain well.

2 Meanwhile, in large bowl, combine dressing ingredients; blend well.

3 Add cooked pasta and all remaining salad ingredients to dressing; stir gently to coat. Serve immediately, or cover and refrigerate until serving time.

1 SERVING

Calories 330 (Calories from Fat 130);
Total Fat 15g (Saturated Fat 3g);
Cholesterol 15mg; Sodium 1,060mg;
Total Carbohydrates 42g (Dietary
Fiber 9g); Sugars 7g; Protein 14g

% Daily Value: Vitamin A 15%;
Vitamin C 45%; Calcium 15%; Iron 20%

Exchanges: 2 Starch, 1 Very Lean Meat,
3 Fat

Carbohydrate Choices: 2

QUICK FIX

Serve this salad with quick-to-fix focaccia wedges. Top a focaccia with roasted red pepper strips from a jar and shredded mozzarella cheese. Broil just until the cheese melts. Cut into wedges and enjoy!

Creamy Pasta-Bean Salad

Mostaccioli—Kidney Bean Salad

■ ■ ■ Ready in 25 minutes

4 servings (1 1/2 cups each)

Salad
1 1/2 cups uncooked mostaccioli pasta (5 oz.)
1 can (15 or 15.5 oz.) dark red kidney beans, drained, rinsed
1/2 medium zucchini, sliced (1 cup)
1 small red bell pepper, cut into strips
1 small tomato, cut into wedges
1/2 cup shredded Parmesan cheese (2 oz.)

Dressing
1/4 cup white wine vinegar
1/4 cup olive oil
4 teaspoons chopped fresh or 1 1/4 teaspoons dried dill
1/2 teaspoon dry mustard
1/4 teaspoon salt
1/8 teaspoon pepper
1 garlic clove, minced or 1/8 teaspoon garlic powder

1. Cook mostaccioli as directed on package. Drain; rinse with cold water to cool. Drain well.
2. Meanwhile, in large bowl, combine dressing ingredients; mix well.
3. Add cooked mostaccioli and all remaining salad ingredients to dressing; toss gently. Serve immediately, or cover and refrigerate until serving time.

1 SERVING

Calories 410 (Calories from Fat 170);
Total Fat 19g (Saturated Fat 4g);
Cholesterol 10mg; Sodium 490mg;
Total Carbohydrates 45g (Dietary
Fiber 6g); Sugars 4g; Protein 15g

% Daily Value: Vitamin A 20%;
Vitamin C 35%; Calcium 20%; Iron 15%

Exchanges: 3 Starch, 1 Very Lean Meat,
3 Fat

Carbohydrate Choices: 2 1/2

QUICK FIX

A small jar with a tight-fitting lid is great to have on hand to mix quick salad dressings. Just add the ingredients to the jar, screw on the lid and shake until blended.

Wild Rice and Bean Salad

Ready in 20 minutes

4 servings (2 cups each)

Dressing
1/4 cup olive oil
1/4 cup vinegar
1 teaspoon dry mustard
1/2 teaspoon salt
1/2 teaspoon pepper
2 garlic cloves, minced or 1/4 teaspoon garlic powder

Salad
1 package (10 oz.) frozen cooked wild rice, thawed,
    or 2 cups cold cooked wild rice
1 can (15 oz.) great northern beans, drained, rinsed
1 can (15 oz.) black beans, drained, rinsed
1 can (4.5 oz.) chopped green chiles
1 medium stalk celery, sliced (1/2 cup)
1 small onion, chopped (1/3 cup)
1/4 cup chopped fresh cilantro
4 cups mixed salad greens

1. In large bowl, combine all dressing ingredients; blend well.
2. Add all salad ingredients except salad greens; toss gently to coat. Arrange salad greens on individual serving plates; spoon wild rice mixture onto greens.

1 SERVING

Calories 200 (Calories from Fat 50);
Total Fat 6g (Saturated Fat 1g);
Cholesterol 0mg; Sodium 440mg;
Total Carbohydrates 31g (Dietary
Fiber 7g); Sugars 3g; Protein 10g

% Daily Value: Vitamin A 15%;
Vitamin C 15%; Calcium 10%; Iron 20%

Exchanges: 1 1/2 Starch, 1 Very Lean Meat,
1 Fat

Carbohydrate Choices: 1 1/2

QUICK FIX

You can use 1/2 cup of your favorite Italian salad dressing instead of making the dressing. And this salad is also good using 2 cups cold cooked brown or white rice instead of the wild rice.

Index

Page numbers in *italics* indicate illustrations